Reimagining Administrative Justice

Margaret Doyle • Nick O'Brien

Reimagining Administrative Justice

Human Rights in Small Places

palgrave
macmillan

Margaret Doyle
University of Essex
London, UK

Nick O'Brien
University of Liverpool
Stockport, UK

ISBN 978-3-030-21387-9 ISBN 978-3-030-21388-6 (eBook)
https://doi.org/10.1007/978-3-030-21388-6

This Palgrave Pivot imprint is published by the registered company Springer Nature Switzerland AG
The registered company address is: Gewerbestrasse 11, 6330 Cham, Switzerland

In memory of:
Dorothy Doyle (1929–2018) and James Doyle (1927–2002)
Maureen O'Brien (1925–1995) and Daniel O'Brien (1919–2009)

Preface

This book comes from the head and from the heart: it is the result of personal experience and reflection. We have been involved in the worlds of administrative justice and human rights as researchers and practitioners in the UK for many years. We have observed developments in both with mixed feelings, optimistic at times and at other times despondent. We are conscious that administrative justice is at a turning point now. It is exciting that new literature is exploring themes such as decision-making, digitalisation, and public inquiries from fresh perspectives. Public scandals like the Grenfell Tower fire, the Windrush generation, and Hillsborough have brought these issues to national attention and highlighted the interaction between social rights and administrative justice, giving scope to a richer understanding of the citizen-and-state relationship. Challenges such as the reform of social security benefits with the introduction of Universal Credit illustrate the links between poverty and a political agenda of austerity. Long-awaited reform of the Westminster and England public sector ombuds has stalled and looks set to be disappointingly unambitious.

It is therefore timely to contribute an intellectual challenge to settled thinking. Our established ways of looking at administrative justice have not brought about the change needed in these times. This book is an attempt to put forward a constructive, perhaps unexpected, vision. It draws on design culture and connects administrative justice in particular with developments in post-war planning, housing and the public realm more generally. It is also an attempt to forge an alliance between social rights and administrative justice, which have for the most part been ships that pass in the night.

The book makes no claim to be an empirical study or comprehensive analysis of the field, but instead constitutes an invitation to further exploration. It is in the spirit of the urban explorer, or *flaneur/flaneuse*, that we have engaged with the issues, and it is with the receptiveness of the *bricoleur* that we have responded to the environment and incorporated unexpected metaphors that we believe assist in the task of creative reimagining. We offer this book quite simply as a prompt to further deliberative discussion—open, inclusive and receptive to many voices.

London, UK Margaret Doyle
Stockport, UK Nick O'Brien

Acknowledgements

We would like to thank the following people for their valuable comments on drafts of this book: Brian Thompson, Naomi Creutzfeldt, Nazia Latif, Oliver Marshall, and Poornima O'Brien.

Contents

Abbreviations

AJTC	Administrative Justice and Tribunals Council
CAJTW	Committee for Administrative Justice and Tribunals Wales
CEDR	Centre for Effective Dispute Resolution
EHRC	Equality and Human Rights Commission
HMCTS	Her Majesty's Courts and Tribunals Service
ILPA	Immigration Law Practitioners Group
LGO	Local Government Ombudsman
LGSCO	Local Government and Social Care Ombudsman
MOJ	Ministry of Justice
MOP	Modern Ombudsman Practice
NAO	National Audit Office
NPM	New Public Management
NIHRC	Northern Ireland Human Rights Commission
NIO	Northern Ireland Ombudsman
NIPSO	Northern Ireland Public Services Ombudsman
OIA	Office of the Independent Adjudicator
PACAC	Public Administration and Constitutional Affairs Select Committee
PASC	Public Administration Select Committee
PHSO	Parliamentary and Health Service Ombudsman
PSOW	Public Services Ombudsman for Wales
SEND	Special educational needs and disabilities
SPSO	Scottish Public Services Ombudsman
UDHR	Universal Declaration of Human Rights
UKAJI	UK Administrative Justice Institute

CHAPTER 1

Introduction

Abstract This chapter introduces the main argument of the book. It recognises that administrative justice and human rights are not commonly considered together. It suggests, however, that the 'small places' of daily life are where both concepts can be located in fruitful alliance. To achieve that alliance, it is necessary to recover the social democratic and post-war roots of administrative justice and human rights, and to trace the unravelling of that social democratic heritage by a dominant neoliberalism that has privileged the notions of individual 'user', 'system', and 'closure' as the settled orthodoxies. The chapter identifies the key role of 'legalism' in that process and recommends instead a 'demosprudential' future in which the concepts of 'community', 'network' and 'openness' emerge as alternative foundations.

Keywords Administrative justice • Human rights • Social democracy • Neoliberalism • Legalism • Demosprudence

The Citizen and the State in a Small Place

At the end of *The Bookshop*, a novel by Penelope Fitzgerald set in late 1950s small-town East Suffolk, England, the main character, Florence Green, is defeated by a lack of administrative justice. She has worked hard against local opposition to establish a bookshop in the Old House, a small historic building that has been empty and mould-ridden for years. Despite

M. Doyle, N. O'Brien, *Reimagining Administrative Justice*,
https://doi.org/10.1007/978-3-030-21388-6_1

her modest success in enlivening the reading habits of the residents of Hardborough, and despite the shop also being her home, Florence is faced with a compulsory purchase order from the District Council, an action made possible by a Private Bill ushered through Parliament by the MP nephew of a powerful local resident determined to oust Florence and her shop. Advised by her lawyer that 'there can't really be any legal grounds for challenging an administrative decision', and that because '[v]arious Town and Country Planning Acts' rule out compensation in cases where a building's dampness makes it uninhabitable, Florence is left with no choice but to sell her stock to pay off her loan on the Old House and, now homeless, to leave Hardborough with only a suitcase.

Not long before Florence Green opened her bookshop, the Franks Committee on Administrative Tribunals and Inquiries completed its inquiry into the ways of challenging government decision making (including on compulsory purchase). The Committee's Report, published in 1957, described the task it had undertaken as one of finding a reasonable balance between what it saw as competing conceptions of 'administrative' and 'judicial' procedures and conflicting interests of Ministers and administrative authorities, on the one hand, and 'the rights and feelings of individual citizens who find their possessions or plans interfered with by the administration' on the other—and indeed a third conflicting interest, the public interest in good administration.

Franks was part of that post-war social democratic moment which emerged against a background of shared faith in the activist state, economic planning and large-scale public investment. Speaking of the 'apogee of the European state' in the 1960s, historian of post-war Europe Tony Judt has remarked, 'The state, then, was a good thing; and there was a lot of it' (Judt 2005: 360, 361). Administrative justice is deeply implicated with those post-war concerns, with the democratic construction of the public realm, with public trust and public meaning. It is implicated too with many of the most pressing social concerns of the modern democratic state and, as a result, with human rights, especially of a social or 'relational' kind, to do with health, social care, education and social housing.

It is in the small places of ordinary daily life, like those of *The Bookshop*, that human rights and administrative justice matter most, and where they share common roots as a political response to the post-war social democratic moment. Their scope and reach are much larger therefore than any narrow identification with the legal process. Their primary focus is nothing less than the relationship between the citizen and the state, between citizen and citizen, and the social meaning of democratic values rooted in the principle of equality. Their future, as this book seeks to show, is unavoidably demosprudential, in the sense that they are concerned with making response to citizen grievance more democratic and with embedding legal change in the broader culture.

The Seductive Embrace of Neoliberalism

Human rights and administrative justice are unfamiliar partners. Whereas human rights have connotations of gravity and fundamental value and the backing of international conventions, administrative justice evokes a sense of dusty proceduralism, in the shadows and with merely contingent significance. They occupy different territory: human rights are associated with substantive civil and political entitlements and with rights enforcement in courts; administrative justice is concerned with the bureaucracy of the state and with procedural fairness.

This book aims to reunite these separate concepts and enhance both as instruments of social justice. It does so by challenging the assumption that they occupy different territory and instead prioritising alternative characterisations of each: social rights, instead of exclusively civil and political rights; administrative justice as a set of principles for shaping humane relationships between citizen and state, instead of the more narrow conception of procedural fairness in decision making. It reconsiders both human rights and administrative justice in relation to response to grievance by proposing that investigation, not adjudication, is the vehicle for a set of practices that are in themselves democratic and that also foster democratic values in the relationship between citizen and state. By rediscovering human rights in the small places of social rights promotion and protection, the book aims to reimagine administrative justice and its democratic reach.

The reference to 'small places' in the title evokes Eleanor Roosevelt's speech to the United Nations in 1958, in which she stated that the origins of human rights can be found in those small, forgotten places, close to home, which do not appear on any map yet which are the world of the individual person and her striving for equal justice, equal opportunity and equal dignity without discrimination. These small places are not for the most part the scene of international politics and law, of war and peace, or of crime and punishment. Instead, they are the small places of social rights entitlement and, in the words of social reformer William Beveridge, the places where the struggle is fought against the social evils of want, disease, ignorance, squalor and idleness. They are the small places also of administrative justice, far away from the court system and the majesty of the law, and instead located at or near street-level—the school, the Job Centre, the hospital. In these small places, as Eleanor Roosevelt astutely observed, the central value is equality. Administrative justice and human rights, properly construed, emphasise egalitarian rather than libertarian values, and they are relational more than individualistic. It is their egalitarian and relational character that invests them with their democratic credentials.

The potential connection between human rights and administrative justice has not passed entirely unnoticed. Too often, however, its importance has been marginalised. Grenfell, Windrush, Hillsborough—these and other tragedies bring into sharp focus the necessary partnership of social rights and the actions of the state. In the wake of national tragedy or public scandal, human rights are invoked and the lack of administrative justice remarked upon, but only after the event and with a sense of surprise. In its investigation into the human rights implications of the 2017 Grenfell Tower fire, for example, the Equality and Human Rights Commission is exploring whether a duty on government to have due regard to the socio-economic impact of its decisions, had it been in force, would have made any difference to what happened, and whether a stronger socio-economic duty is required. Administrative justice institutions, such as ombuds, tribunals and mediation, from time to time emphasise their role as part of the national human-rights structures, but rarely very loudly or for very long. For the most part, human rights and administrative justice are ships that pass in the night.

This book seeks to explain this sense of alienation and to propose a remedy. It does so by identifying administrative justice as the product of what Tony Judt identified as the post-war 'social democratic moment', closely implicated with that moment's largely positive evaluation of the state, prioritisation of equality (at least in theory) and celebration of the public realm. At that time, from the late 1940s into the 1960s, a political and cultural consensus emerged that stands in stark contrast to the neoliberal epoch which has largely prevailed in the West since the early 1970s. Over time, however, a strong strain of libertarianism and suspicion of state bureaucracy and control made administrative justice receptive to the values of individualism and consumerism and ripe for conversion to the cause of neoliberalism. In legal-theoretical terms, its legisprudential origins, based on a primary relationship with the legislature, gave way to a jurisprudential maturity in which individual rights, especially property, financial and privacy rights, and a narrowing court-based conception of the rule of law, held sway.

Human rights are the product of that same post-war social democratic moment, and they too shared in the positive evaluation of the democratic state, the prioritisation of equality and celebration of the public realm. They too in time fell for the seductive embrace of neoliberalism and became associated with individualism and consumerism and with the dominant value of individual liberty and market-choice. Social and relational rights became devalued, to the extent that they were hardly thought to be human rights at all. The legisprudential foundation of human rights in constitutional value gave way to a jurisprudential future in which adjudication and enforcement became the hallmarks of individual entitlement. What began as forces for democratic value and equality have ended up, albeit unwittingly, as the agents of an impoverished form of individualism and of market-triumphalism.

Problematic Orthodoxies: 'User', 'System', 'Closure'

How is it then that administrative justice, despite its promise, finds itself relegated to the margins as a 'Cinderella', painted into a corner that at times seems very dusty? Two mentalities have contributed to that process of marginalisation, in a way that mirrors the similar marginalisation of social rights: legalism and consumerism. 'Law's Empire' (Dworkin 1986) has proved hard to resist. Academic commentators had noted with dismay the judicialisation of the tribunal system even before its absorption within HM Courts and Tribunals Service in 2007. At the same time, the public ombud institution in and across the UK, although conceived as chalk to the cheese of the legal process, has largely acquiesced in an individualistic and legalistic 'dispute resolution' function. Associated with the orthodoxy that the resolution of individual disputes is the model of any institutional response to citizen grievance, there is a creeping mentality of consumerism, more recently incestuously married to its sibling New Public Management, and its values of efficiency, effectiveness and economy, that has effectively impoverished the conception of citizenship (and of 'social citizenship', in particular) and of what a response to citizen grievance might be.

There are, as a result, three orthodoxies that, although taken to typify the essential design features of administrative justice, invite scrutiny: the priority of 'the user', the desirability of 'system', and the inevitability of 'closure'.

The priority of the individual user has become sacrosanct in current debate about the design of administrative justice. Reflecting the consumerist ambition that the individual 'user' of any service or process is the invariable point of reference, so that 'user friendliness' becomes its most salient characteristic, proposals for redesign of administrative justice have increasingly taken it for granted that any response to citizen grievance should be judged by how effectively it offers 'satisfaction' to the individual 'user', whether in accessing a tribunal, first-instance decision-maker, mediator or ombud. Yet there are grounds for scepticism about the wisdom of such prioritisation, not because the user is unimportant but because the true identity of 'the user' is frequently contested, rarely simple, and never a matter of purely individual choice, divorced from all social and shared need.

Secondly, it has become commonplace to construct a discussion of the administrative justice 'system' around the preliminary observation that, in contrast to the criminal justice, family justice or civil justice systems, the administrative justice system does not as yet exist, and moreover that this is a bad thing. The desirability of making administrative justice more 'systematic', in the sense of more clearly structured and bounded, with practice and process more uniformly prescribed and co-ordinated, the 'user journey' more transparently 'mapped' for ease of passage and certainty of destination, has become a cherished ideal.

This striving for systematisation, for consistency and certainty, looks dubious as an overarching strategy, not least because it fails to take account of the unavoidability of uncertainty and the need to remain 'agile' in the face of an unpredictable future. Too much 'system' can lead to precisely the uniformity, bureaucracy and inflexibility (associated so often with the legal system) that administrative justice has always aspired to counter. Instead, it is worth recasting administrative justice as less of a system and more of a woven fabric, to look for what Bauhaus weaver Anni Albers described in 1958 as the 'interdependent threads' that, when connected, 'form a cohesive and flexible whole' (Albers 1965).

Finally, the emphasis on individual redress has reinforced the expectation, derived from the common law mentality, that any serious attempt to respond to citizen grievance must aim for finality and 'closure'. Even if the outcome is one of disappointment for the individual complainant, at least the administrative justice process will have brought things to an end, achieved closure and so enabled the individual 'to move on'. On this account, 'business as usual' is the desired result, the public trial the paradigm of theatrical denouement.

Yet the prescription of closure as a worthwhile policy ambition for administrative justice is far from straightforward. To design for closure is to design for resignation, for the acceptance of limit and definition, for boundary and exclusivity. The ability of administrative justice to engage in iterative practices, deliver provisional outcomes, and enable future creative participation, albeit under the shadow of inevitable uncertainty, is by such an ambition seriously constrained.

In search of a remedy, this book looks to the culture of design to identify alternatives to these three problematic orthodoxies, and in particular to the design culture that emerged also as part of the social democratic moment and that has been shaped since then by similar forces to those shaping the cultures of human rights and administrative justice. The response to those forces, as illustrated in current thinking on urban design, provides useful pointers to a way to reimagine human rights and administrative justice as necessary partners.

Designing a Demosprudential Future: 'Community', 'Network' and 'Openness'

Design theory has somewhat belatedly made a self-conscious entry into discussion about the future of administrative justice. The prospects of a future that is 'digital by default' have made more pressing a measure of critical reflection on what design might mean for administrative justice, and indeed for the fabric of the justice system more generally. The trajectory of design culture since 1945 and its own entanglements with democratic value, individualism and the marketplace are instructive, not only because of its exposure to similar pressures as those exerted on administrative justice and human rights but because of the emergence in design culture of innovative and progressive solutions that seek to valorise democratic values and equality. Part of the purpose of this book is to explore the resonance between design culture and the reconnection of human rights with administrative justice, and so assert their abiding kinship as proponents of a reinvigorated democracy.

At the heart of the book's argument is the proposition that, in the case of both human rights and administrative justice, design features shaped by essentially legalistic values of 'individual user', 'system' and 'closure' have obscured their shared roots in democratic value and impaired their democratic potential. Illustration from the broader design culture underpins that proposition and seeks to make concrete the process of reimagining that the book invites. It is in the design of the public realm, in urban planning and housing development that the values that can shape a reinvigorated democracy become most clearly visible and in which the possibilities for administrative justice and human rights emerge most clearly. Drawing on current design thinking, we identify the alternative values of 'community' (rather than individual user), 'network' (as opposed to system) and 'openness' (instead of closure). Using these alternatives and the reorientation they invite, the book aims to show how administrative justice can be reimagined not as a landscape or a system but as a 'fabric', something woven and rough-edged, made by human hand and touch, and to show how its small places can be sanctuary for a human rights discourse that is social, egalitarian and relational rather than individualistic, libertarian, and atomised. It seeks to do that by focusing in particular on the ombud, as the paradigm institution of administrative justice and as the potential purveyor of a form of investigation that allows the most scope for putting those alternative values into practice.

In place of the legisprudential and jurisprudential past, the book advocates a demosprudential future. Demosprudence is a term coined to denote practices that build on the ability of social movements or mobilized communities to make, interpret and change the law. As such, demosprudence is a vehicle for democratizing the process of responding to citizen grievance and embedding legal change in broader cultural transformation. It is a reaction against those forms of legalism that embrace a common law mentality of strict legal precedent, command-and-control enforcement, adversarialism and individualism, and strict separation of law from ethics, culture and politics. It achieves that aim by fashioning values and processes that can enable civic participation and create bridges between different interests. It finds resonance in, but is not defined by, related ideas such as public interest law, network governance, democratic experimentalism, legal pragmatism, deliberative democracy, therapeutic justice and problem-solving courts. Through the prioritisation of community, network and openness, demosprudence offers a coherent alternative to practices based on the individual user, system and closure.

In demosprudence, human rights and administrative justice find a common future in the small places of social and relational rights, a future that delivers on their radically democratic potential for responding to citizen grievance. As such, they form part of a broader engagement with democratic values and equality in sustaining a public realm characterised by social innovation and a form of political friendship that can transcend difference.

Bureaucracy is the frontier where the citizen meets the state and feels its texture. The problem in bureaucracy is, in turn, a problem in relationships. Human rights and administrative justice are, in their different ways and common origins, both means of humanising those relationships and investing them with democratic credibility. It is the purpose of this book to suggest how that rapprochement can be realised more effectively.

A Modest Manifesto

The approach advancing this purpose is for the most part analytic and comparative: it is not the purpose of this book to present new empirical evidence or to offer an exhaustive textbook account of the issues under consideration. Furthermore, the perspective adopted is largely that of Westminster government and the English regions, primarily because it is there, within the UK as a whole, that the need for reimagining is most starkly evident. The different and often more progressive experience in Scotland, Wales and Northern Ireland is referred to but not considered in detail. In that sense, this book is intended as what writer Orhan Pamuk has referred to as a 'modest manifesto'—modest only in the sense that it intentionally leaves room for new insights and connections, inviting readers to dig deeper and to 'tell stories on a human scale' (Pamuk 2013).

The book begins by describing, in Chaps. 2 and 3, what administrative justice and human rights are and identifying the origins of each in the post-war social democratic moment. It acknowledges also the gradual erosion of that social democratic vision and infiltration of administrative justice and human rights by neoliberal values, individualism and consumerism in which a legalistic and jurisprudential framework is complicit. Central to the discussion is the emergence of the individual, of system and of closure as the priorities adopted in both administrative justice and human rights and as their central, but highly problematic, values.

Chapter 4 broadens the discussion to include the culture of design, especially as reflected in the emergence of town planning and urban design following World War II but also in the more recent application of design thinking to administrative justice. The consonance between politics and design was celebrated in the Festival of Britain in 1951, which drew much of its inspiration from 'humane' Scandinavian design coupled with nostalgia for a British 'craft past', as exemplified in the rediscovery of William Morris and the distinctive social vision evoked by his name. Design was explicitly part of a broader social vision, a 'tonic to the nation' and in effect 'an aesthetic offshoot of the Welfare State'. The discussion also draws on the design of court buildings to illustrate the tensions between public and private value and on digital justice reform to explore the implications of new technologies. Exploring design culture and its relevance to administrative justice and human rights enables us to chart their social-democratic aspirations and the encroachment upon those aspirations of market values. More positively, Chap. 4 finds in design culture the seeds of a more progressive and democratic reimagining that prioritises community, network and openness over individual user, system and closure.

In Chaps. 5 and 6 the focus shifts to the implications of this potential reimagining for administrative justice and human rights, and in particular for the ombud, with its distinctive techniques and character, as the central institution of administrative justice reimagined. It does so by considering the way in which practices of adjudication, for example in India, have gradually become more investigative and in that way better adapted to make more democratic the engagement of conventional courts with social rights protection and promotion. It also considers how the ombud, for example in Latin America and southern Europe, but also in Britain, has already, in sometimes surprisingly similar ways, extended its reach to make effective its own democratic engagement with social rights and the task of humanising the state bureaucracy.

In Chap. 7, the focus widens to consider the implications of the values of community, network and openness for other parts of the administrative justice fabric, notably mediation, tribunals and public inquiries. The themes of looking and listening are integral to the practices of the institutions of administrative justice when they are reimagined as demosprudential, with a focus on recognition rather than resolution, and as parts of an interlocking network sustained by participative processes.

The concluding Chap. 8 explores the broader political vision compatible with a reimagined administrative justice. By recognising the unavoidably political context of administrative justice and human rights, the discussion touches upon ideas of radical democracy, political friendship and social innovation as a means of threading the ombud as the paradigm of administrative justice to other pieces of the administrative-justice fabric. In that way, administrative justice reimagined becomes an essential component of human rights promotion and protection, and of the democratic state founded on the principle of equality.

* * *

Writing in 1965, political commentator Andrew Shonfield spoke persuasively of public administration as a 'cult of bureaucratic humanity', of 'imagination and kindness' from public officials towards private persons. This book argues that it is possible to reinstate that vision without embarrassment or misplaced idealism. In its most concrete form, such a vision entails that first-instance decision makers, mediators, tribunals and ombud-institutions should not submit to Law's Empire and consumerist values to the extent that they become merely clearance houses for 'small claims', jettisoned by the legal system as an inconvenience for which an 'informal' process represents better value for money. Just as importantly, such a vision entails also that these key non-judicial institutions do not simply mimic the judicial process by adopting unwaveringly the imperatives of individualistic legal liberalism.

The actively benevolent state, as recognised in the 1950s and 1960s, is stuck with 'the problem of bureaucracy'. The 'cult of bureaucratic humanity' and the promotion of trust, however, remain attainable ambitions. It is the purpose of this book to show how those ambitions can be realised in the reimagining of administrative justice quite simply as an instrument of institutional reform, public trust, social rights and political friendship.

References

Albers, A. (1965). *On Weaving*. Middletown, CT: Wesleyan University Press.

Dworkin, R. (1986). *Law's Empire*. London: Fontana.

Judt, T. (2005). *Postwar: A History of Europe since 1945*. London: William Heinemann.

Pamuk, O. (2013, June/July). A Modest Manifesto for Museums. *American Craft Magazine*.

CHAPTER 2

A Social Democratic Vision

Abstract This chapter considers the social democratic origins of post-war administrative justice and human rights. It emphasises the relevance of administrative justice to ordinary daily life and its importance as a set of principles that govern the relationship between individual citizens and the democratic state. It identifies the social rights entitlements to health, social care, education and housing as integral to the post-war human rights vision, and touches upon the way in which the devolved legislatures in Scotland and Wales have begun to reinstate that vision. It proposes the 'relational' character of both administrative justice and human rights as central and a 'duty of active kindness' as critical to their realisation.

Keywords Social democracy • Citizenship • Devolution • Relationship • Kindness

Voices from Small Places: Why Administrative Justice Matters

On 14 June 2017, 71 residents of Grenfell Tower in the London Borough of Kensington and Chelsea died in a fire which swept through the 24-story building in the early hours of the morning (another resident died some months later as a result of her injuries, bringing the final tally to 72).

M. Doyle, N. O'Brien, *Reimagining Administrative Justice*,
https://doi.org/10.1007/978-3-030-21388-6_2

Although managed privately by Kensington & Chelsea Tenant Management Organisation (TMO), the tower block was publicly owned by the Borough Council.

In the years preceding the fire, the Council had been told of residents' concerns: in 2013, the Grenfell Action Group reported anxieties about a fire risk; local councillor Judith Blakeman, also a member of the TMO, expressed concerns about the installation of National Grid gas pipes in the main stairwells; and in January 2016, the former chair of the Residents Association called for an inquiry at a meeting of the Council's housing and planning scrutiny committee.

These local expressions of concern were just one manifestation of broader reservations about national housing policy. In 2013, Raquel Rolnik, then UN-appointed special rapporteur on the right to housing, warned that the UK government's reduction in investment in social housing and the linked concentration instead on the private rental market were having a damaging impact on the availability and suitability of social housing. Subsequently, in April 2016 Ms Rolnik's successor, Leilani Farha, joined with others in reinforcing those human rights (especially social rights) concerns in a communication to the UK government about the effect of austerity measures on housing standards. Similar concerns were also adopted by a UN committee of independent human rights experts who recommended that the UK government take corrective measures as a matter of urgency. As Leilani Farha has since observed (*The Guardian*, 21 June 2017), 'We were all echoing the voices of thousands of residents who had been systematically and repeatedly raising their concerns with their councils and governments'.

Yet the failure of the UK government to heed those voices—its rejection of 'both the message and the messengers' (as Leilani Farha puts it)—has led to the recognition of Grenfell Tower not just as a human tragedy but as a human rights tragedy. In its announcement of its intention to investigate the fire from a human rights and equality perspective, the UK's national human rights institution, the Equality and Human Rights Commission (EHRC), has drawn attention to several possible breaches of the state's duties: to protect the right to life, to prevent inhuman and degrading treatment, to ensure the availability of adequate and safe housing, to provide access to justice to those with grievances before the fire, to protect the rights in particular of children, and to avoid discrimination, make reasonable adjustments for disabled people and have due regard to the need to advance equality of opportunity. Echoing the observations of

Leilani Farha, the EHRC also remarked in its public statement: 'It is critical for the State to ensure that residents' concerns about safety are heard and acted upon. We will consider whether there were proper arrangements for ensuring that residents' voices were heard by those in positions of power' (EHRC 2017).

In the encounter between the citizen and the state, as opposed to that between the consumer and the producer, it is the exercise of 'voice', rather than 'exit' or choice, that remains the primary instrument of accountability (Hirschman 1970). It is here, in the impaired exercise of voice and of public accountability, that the Grenfell Tower fire emerges not just as a human tragedy, or even a human rights tragedy, but as an administrative justice tragedy also. As the UK Administrative Justice Institute (UKAJI) has observed, administrative justice should above all be identified as an 'overarching set of principles and values governing individuals' interactions with the state rather than as being one of the four "strands" of the justice system', alongside the better known criminal, civil and family jurisdictions (UKAJI 2018: 9). In the case of Grenfell Tower, it was the poverty of those interactions between citizen and state, and their failure to conform to any adequate overarching set of principles and values, that set the stage for the tragic human events which unfolded. Administrative justice matters, and the way it matters can be quite simply a matter of life and death.

I, Daniel Blake and the Human Consequences of Administrative Justice

We need look no further than the catalogue of public scandal in the UK in recent years for further illustration of the point, not only Grenfell Tower but Hillsborough, Mid-Staffordshire NHS Trust, Morecombe Bay, the Windrush Generation. These are enough to evoke a trail of human devastation that has at its roots a fundamental breakdown in the relationship between citizen and state, an unremitting inability of citizens to exercise voice effectively and to hold the state to account. At the root of each of these scandals is the failure to ensure that the enduring relationship between individual and public authority is one that is characterised by humane and democratic principle and by the observance of social rights entitlement to 'positive liberty' ('freedom to') through the availability of health care, social care, housing, and education as much as of civil rights entitlements to 'negative liberty' ('freedom from') in its various forms (Berlin 1969).

The human consequences of such breakdown have received powerful treatment also on the cinema screen. Ken Loach's *I, Daniel Blake* (Laverty and Loach 2016) is amongst other things a film about administrative justice, about Daniel Blake's tragic encounters in north-east England with the welfare benefits system and the state bureaucracy that surrounds it. Overwhelmed by an unremitting sequence of appeals and sanctions, Blake, in the first instance defeated by the adjudication of an anonymous 'decision-maker', eventually finds himself at the door of a tribunal, where the film reaches its dramatic conclusion.

On its release, the film elicited contrasting political reactions: praise from Leader of the Labour Party, Jeremy Corbyn; condemnation from Damien Green, then Work and Pensions Secretary, who thought it 'monstrously unfair'. Whatever its merits, at its core the film is nothing less than a depiction of the relationship between the individual and the state and of the apparent lack of any overarching set of principles and values that could be recognised as humane or democratic. Daniel Blake's explicit manifesto, daubed on the wall of a JobCentre, is hardly a polite request for better 'customer care' or less officious staff. It is instead a visceral plea for a renewed sense of 'social citizenship', stripped of any creeping consumerism and clothed instead with a sense of civic dignity:

> *I am not a client, a customer, nor a service user. I am not a shirker, a scrounger, a beggar nor a thief. I am not a national insurance number, nor a blip on a screen. I paid my dues, never a penny short, and proud to do so. I don't tug the forelock but look my neighbour in the eye. I don't accept or seek charity. My name is Daniel Blake, I am a man, not a dog. As such, I demand my rights. I demand you treat me with respect. I, Daniel Blake, am a citizen, nothing more, nothing less. Thank you.*

This reconception of social citizenship, this re-understanding of how humane and democratic values and principles might inform the relationship between individual and state, is the essential material of administrative justice. Although in the past characterised as the 'Cinderella' of the justice system, administrative justice is the canvas on which social citizenship achieves clear definition as daily practice. The day-to-day routines of administrative justice—first-instance decision-making by public authorities, both local and national; the work of tribunals in relation to immigration, welfare benefits, detention in mental hospitals, special educational needs; the deliberative intervention of mediators in disputes with public authorities; and the investigations conducted by ombud-institutions of complaints about healthcare, housing and social care—are the small places where human tragedies, human rights tragedies, unfold. This canvas can reasonably be said to accommodate more than the civil element of citizenship, comprising the rights necessary for individual freedom, or indeed the political element, comprising the right to participate in the exercise of political power. Critically, it also accommodates the social element, influentially described by T.H. Marshall in his 1949 Marshall Lectures at Cambridge as 'the whole range from the right to a modicum of economic welfare and security to the right to share to the full in the social heritage and to live the life of a civilised being according to the standards prevailing in the society' (Marshall 1992: 8); and central to this social element, as Marshall also emphasised, is 'an urge towards a fuller measure of equality' (Marshall 1992: 18). The administrative justice vision is to that extent ambitiously egalitarian rather than merely libertarian in its reach.

Small Places on a Large Scale

The sheer scale of administrative justice interactions, in small places, is a further measure of this reach. As Lord Newton, a former chair of the Council on Tribunals, suggested to the House of Lords in 2010, administrative justice, despite its low profile, is arguably more important to ordinary citizens than either civil or family justice (Newton 2010). The annual volume of administrative justice 'transactions' is considerable: for example, the Department for Work and Pensions (DWP) makes 12 million social security decisions per year, leading to 300,000 Mandatory Reconsiderations and 150,000 tribunal appeals; millions of decisions are made on immigration and tax by the Home Office and HM Revenue and Customs respectively, leading to a further 57,000 tribunal appeals (Thomas and Tomlinson 2017). Local authorities in England make 339,000 appealable decisions on special educational needs (SEN) each year (Ministry of Justice 2017). In 2017–18, 32,000 complaints were handled by the UK Parliamentary Ombudsman and Health Service Ombudsman for England and 19,000 by the Local Government and Social Care Ombudsman (PHSO 2018; LGSCO 2018). Just as significantly, the rate of success in challenging first-instance decisions is high: 67% of appeals against DWP decisions were decided in favour of the claimant (including 71% for some benefits) (Ministry of Justice 2018);

50% of appeals against Home Office decisions on immigration were granted (including 59% of human rights appeals) (Ministry of Justice 2018); 89% of appeals decided on special educational needs were in favour of the appellant (Ministry of Justice 2017).

Furthermore, administrative justice, even routinely, touches upon events critical to daily life. As Richard Thomas, the last chair of the Administrative Justice and Tribunals Council (AJTC), observed towards the end of his tenure in 2011, at any one moment those engaged with administrative justice are likely to include the asylum seeker, the incapacity benefit claimant, the mental patient seeking discharge from detention in hospital, the widowed spouse of a war veteran fighting for a pension, the teenager permanently excluded from school, the police officer dismissed for alleged misconduct and the doctor refused registration by the National Health Service (Thomas 2011). They also include the driver who is issued a parking penalty and the landowner applying for planning permission. These are the small places where the day-to-day dramas of administrative justice are played out.

Sometimes too those small places generate very large consequences. On 17 December 2010 Mohamed Bouazizi set fire to himself beside the town hall of Sidi Bouzid in Tunisia after being refused a street-trade licence by the municipal authorities. Eighteen days later he was dead of his injuries. By then the Arab Spring was in the air. In his novel based on Bouazizi's story, Tahar Ben Jelloun remarks:

> *I had never heard about the small town of Sidi Bouzid. Yet, it's here that it all started. Even though the incident was common and banal, this time it ended by triggering the irrevocable.* (Ben Jelloun 2016: 13)

Ben Jelloun's words recall those of Eleanor Roosevelt on the origins of universal human rights in those small, forgotten places, close to home (Roosevelt 1958). Mohamed Bouazizi's struggle for administrative justice occurred in such an environment, marked by police corruption and bureaucratic indifference. When he refused to pay the expected bribe to the police for his licence, Bouazizi was, in Ben Jelloun's words, exposed to 'supreme humiliation', reduced to the condition of 'a slave', so that 'his face is no longer visible, his eyes can no longer see', and, we might add, his voice cannot be heard: like the residents of Grenfell Tower, he took his grievance to the local authorities but he could not be heard above the din of corruption and of bureaucratic insensibility.

Administrative Justice: A Return to the Shadows

Not so long ago it seemed that the business of looking for administrative justice and seeing it in plain view was about to become easier than ever before. In 2010 it was asserted confidently, and persuasively, that administrative justice was 'emerging from the shadows' (Adler 2010: xv). Whereas for so long the term 'administrative justice' had been 'shrouded in obscurity', recent developments in public policy finally heralded a brighter dawn. The report of the Leggatt Review, 'Tribunals for Users—One system, one service' (2001), the White Paper 'Complaints, Redress and Tribunals' (2004) and the Tribunals, Courts and Enforcement Act (2007) had for the first time given impetus to official recognition of the need for a more 'integrated' or 'holistic' approach to administrative justice. Instead of viewing public administration exclusively from the top-down perspective of administrative law (with its emphasis on separate institutions such as courts, tribunals, public inquiries and ombuds), or exclusively from the bottom-up perspective of 'street-level bureaucracy' and first-instance decision making, this new integrated approach appeared to acknowledge the potentially virtuous feedback loop that existed between administrative law and 'justice in administration'. The institutional recognition of that integrated vision took material form in the new AJTC, which in 2007 replaced the much narrower Council on Tribunals, as the 'hub of the wheel of administrative justice' (Leggatt 2001).

The 2004 White Paper, in particular, had identified a new way forward by, for the first time in more than a generation, setting out a vision for administrative justice that aimed to give it parity with civil and family justice: it spoke ambitiously of an administrative justice 'system' that would co-ordinate not just courts and tribunals but ombuds and departmental first-instance decision-makers; it proposed as the guiding principle for the construction of this system the principle of 'proportionate dispute resolution'; and it elevated the individual 'user' to a position of pre-eminence at the expense of judges and officials for whose benefit and convenience other parts of the 'justice system' had so often seemed to be organised.

Just two years later, however, after the optimistic assertion that administrative justice was emerging from the shadows, in 2012 the same author (Adler 2012) reluctantly offered an international audience a very different and 'cautionary' tale of the 'rise and fall' of administrative justice in the UK. Not only had the AJTC already been listed for abolition in the new Conservative and Liberal Democrat Coalition Government's 'bonfire of the quangos' in 2010, but tribunals, with their aspiration towards distinctive non-judicial ways of working, had been merged with the courts in the new HM Courts and Tribunals Service. The prediction was stark: the pendulum set in motion by the Leggatt Review had already fallen, and 'the shaft of light which fell on administrative justice' was now likely to presage 'its renewed eclipse by civil justice' (Adler 2012: 54).

The swing of the pendulum is illustrated by administrative justice policy. Although policy had become less ad hoc in the first decade of the twenty-first century, the failure of successive governments to fully pursue the logic of any model of administrative justice has led to a decrease rather than increase in access to justice since 2010 (Mullen 2017). The effects of the government's austerity agenda include the failure to pursue a holistic vision of administrative justice, significant cuts to legal aid and efforts to weaken judicial review and rights of appeal. Attributing these entirely to austerity policies is perhaps misguided, however: it is not always straightforward establishing economic circumstances, as opposed to political will, as the cause of changes that might just as well have been introduced by a government taking office in more favourable economic conditions (Mullen 2017). More concerning is that the lack of will to transform administrative justice along the lines proposed by the AJTC, and in particular its focus on 'right first time', has resulted in a 'system' that resembles an ever-busy assembly line of complaints and appeals rather than the 'learning machine' focused on improvement, as envisaged by the AJTC.

Relational Rights and the Social-Democratic Moment

An essay in the 2010 collection mentioned above offered a preliminary estimation of the impact of human rights law on administrative justice since the passing of the Human Rights Act 1998 and the sign-off of the EU Fundamental Charter of Human Rights in the Treaty of Lisbon in 2007 (Feldman 2010). The author's conclusion was that human rights law now had an impact on each of the orthodox models of administrative justice (bureaucratic rationality; professional treatment; moral judgment; managerialism, consumerism and markets) identified separately by socio-legal scholars Jerry Mashaw and Michael Adler: human rights law affects the extent to which the systematic and bureaucratic needs of an organisation can be the primary focus of decision-making; it constrains discretion in identifying and meeting people's needs; it restricts the range of what counts as substantive fairness; and it provides constraints on acceptable outcomes in respect of managerialism, consumerism and markets respectively.

The main import of human rights 'is likely to be as side-constraints' (Feldman 2010)—constraints on the range of values which can be pursued, on the methods used to pursue them, on the types of accountability needed, and on the justifications for infringement of those rights that are admissible in law. In this way, legal sanction to protect rights 'can be seen as increasing the weight attributable to rights in comparison with bureaucratic rationality, markets, and so on' (Feldman 2010: 106). In other words, judgements about what is acceptable in administrative justice contexts must be measured against human rights legislation.

There is, however, urgent need for an even broader approach to the impact and importance of human rights for administrative justice, and indeed of administrative justice for human rights. Such an approach entails engagement more with the 'culture' or 'mentality' of human rights as an instrument for promoting social citizenship and equality than with human rights law as a vehicle primarily for protecting individual liberty, and with the implications of that culture for the specific issue of administrative justice design. By locating the emergence of contemporary administrative justice in the post-war social democratic moment, it is possible to uncover the social citizenship roots, and potential, of administrative justice and to water those roots by reference to various motifs drawn from the development of thinking and practice in design more generally.

The context of administrative justice, and indeed of human rights, extends more broadly to the 'small places' of social and cultural encounter, and indeed to a vision of human rights that is more 'social' and 'relational' than the dominant approach with its decisively individualistic tendencies and focus on enforcement of individual rights: 'Rights are traditionally seen as attached to individuals and promoting individual rights such as autonomy and privacy, aimed at keeping people separate and free. These are seen to promote an individualist conception of people' (Herring 2017: 165). This individualist tendency is at odds with the daily experience of ordinary life as 'relational'. The 'relational' aspects of administrative justice as primarily to do with the relationship between the individual and the state find resonance also in the potentially 'relational' aspects of social rights entitlement, with its emphasis on positive duties rather than negative restraints, and on the universal needs of human communities rather than the 'episodic choices' of individuals.

Design Decisions in a Devolved Context

In the UK, devolution of governance in Scotland and Wales has provided fresh opportunity to re-embed relational and social rights in a series of integrated and innovative approaches to administrative justice. In Wales, for example, the link between administrative justice and social justice was established in the 2016 legacy report of the Committee for Administrative Justice and Tribunals in Wales, and although this link was not made explicit in subsequent legislation for tribunal reform, there is evidence of a distinctively Welsh approach to administrative justice that incorporates social rights. As a result, Wales has been described as 'a jurisdiction at the forefront of contemporary movements that are more rights-based and designed to engage citizens, at a time when traditional notions of the administrative state are facing a legitimacy crisis' (Nason 2018). It has even been proposed that the Welsh Government should adopt a policy for administrative justice in Wales 'which draws explicit connections between administrative justice, and issues of human rights, equality, public services and local government reform in Wales, and includes principles of administrative justice redress design' (Nason 2018: 17).

That the focus is not only on rights of the individual but on collective rights is reflected in the growth of the 'integrity branch' of the constitution in Wales. The Welsh Assembly has established not only the first Children's Commissioner in the UK, but also commissioners for older people, for Welsh language, and most recently for 'Future Generations', under the Well-being of Future Generations (Wales) Act 2015. The Act requires public bodies to respect five explicit principles when implementing sustainable development: long-termism, integration, involvement, collaboration, and prevention. As a result, 'Co-operation, involvement, co-decision and co-production in the design of the administrative state and the services it provides' are keywords: 'The Welsh ways of working emphasise horizontal accountability (inter-institutional accountability), enabling citizen participation and furthering opportunities for deliberative democracy' (Nason 2018: 30).

In Scotland, a policy commitment by the Government to embed social rights in devolved administrative justice is delivered in the Social Security (Scotland) Act 2018. The intention, reflecting the aim to create a 'fairer Scotland', is to ground the administration of devolved welfare benefits (mostly related to disability and sickness benefits) in a framework that acknowledges the entitlement to social security as a human right. A key principle of the framework is that 'social security is itself a human right and essential to the realisation of other human rights' (O'Cinneide 2018).

Human Rights: Social Democracy and Culture

It was on 27 March 1958 that, in the course of remarks to the United Nations, Eleanor Roosevelt, one of the chief architects of the Universal Declaration of Human Rights in 1948, observed:

> *Where, after all, do universal human rights begin? In small places, close to home—so close and so small that they cannot be seen on any maps of the world. Yet they are the world of the individual person; the neighbourhood he (sic) lives in; the school or college he attends; the factory, farm or office where he works.* (Roosevelt 1958)

Her observation, frequently cited since as affirmation of the sheer ordinariness of human rights in action, effectively distances the Universal Declaration from any sort of legalistic interpretation, which might instead seek to associate human rights exclusively, or even predominantly, with high matters of state, with international courts, criminal violation or fundamental freedoms from state intrusion and surveillance. As she had remarked earlier, in her 1940 publication *The Moral Basis of Democracy*, 'Court decisions and laws and government administration are just the results of the way people progress inwardly' (Roosevelt 2016).

Such disassociation is consistent with the views variously expressed by the other chief framers of the Universal Declaration: Rene Cassin, for example, observed that, 'In the eyes of the Declaration's authors, effective respect for human rights depends primarily and above all on the mentalities of individuals and social groups' (Cassin 1972); Charles Malik, writing in 1968, noted that 'Men (sic), cultures and natures must first mature inwardly before there can be effective international machinery to adjudicate complaints about the violation of human rights' (Malik 1968); and Peng-chun Chang, having cited a Chinese proverb to the effect that 'Laws alone are not sufficient to bring about results themselves', went on to describe the Universal Declaration's chief goal as 'to build up better human beings, and not merely punish those who violate human rights' (Glendon 2001).

This apparently shared prioritisation of 'culture' over 'law' reflects too the hope expressed by Eleanor Roosevelt contemporaneously with the promulgation of the Universal Declaration in 1948 that it should be 'frankly educational' in demonstrating to a world audience that a sense of personal security and dignity depends upon certain protections (Roosevelt 1948). Such protections, however, are not simply the traditional negative freedoms from state intrusion encapsulated by the banner of civil and political rights, but the positive expectation of the state that it will protect the individual person from 'want', by ensuring the provision of social rights entitlement in the form of adequate housing, health care, food, social care, education and social insurance.

Such sentiments express the direct influence on Mrs Roosevelt not so much of the Second World War but of the Great Depression and the New Deal. Indeed, President Roosevelt's 'Four Freedoms Speech' in 1941 played a crucial role in determining the content of the Universal Declaration, in particular by recognising 'freedom from want' as fundamental. Such content, critically, includes the sort of positive social rights entitlements set out in what American jurist Cass Sunstein calls 'America's Second Bill of Rights' unveiled by President Roosevelt's second inaugural speech on 11 January 1944 and comprising rights to a job, food and clothing, to a decent living, decent homes, medical care and good health, to protection from the economic fears of old age, sickness, accident or unemployment, and to good education (Sunstein 2004). This interdependence in the Universal Declaration of civil and more 'relational' social rights helps frame the educational, and indeed evangelical, ambition of the Declaration, with its prioritisation of culture over law, and its recognition of positive obligations on the state to deliver a range of social goods as well as abstain from the infringement of personal liberties. The contemporary and practical consequences of that insight were already apparent in the emerging post-war independence struggles in Africa and Asia. As B. R. Ambedkar, the legal member of India's pre-independence constituent assembly and chief framer of its 1950 Constitution, noted in 1949, equal political recognition would be largely meaningless without social equality to match, thereby leading to a 'republic of contradictions':

> *In politics we will have equality, and in social and economic life we will have inequality. In politics, we will be recognising the principle of 'one man, one vote' (sic) and 'one vote, one value'. In our social and economic life, we shall by reasons of our social and economic structure, continue to deny the principle of 'one man, one value' (sic). How long shall we continue to live this life of contradictions? How long shall we continue to deny equality in our social and economic life?.* (Ambedkar 2010)

To that extent, the Universal Declaration encompasses egalitarian as well as libertarian values, the social-democratic goal of 'free and equal citizenship' rather than the exaltation of negative individual liberty and mere 'status equality'. A human rights charter is, in the words of Conor Gearty's 2005 Hamlyn Lectures, more 'mission statement' than conventional legal instrument, and it is a charter for the achievement of relational rights and social citizenship more than merely individual civil rights in isolation from a broader communitarian vision (Gearty 2006). Yet within a year of its promulgation, the integrated vision of the Universal Declaration had been split apart by the separate covenants of civil and political rights and of socio-economic rights respectively, the former enforceable in an international court, the latter subject to committee oversight and unenforceable recommendation. The pattern for worldwide separation between civil and social rights had been established, with consequences that still resonate for the way in which human rights are perceived and given effect.

Administrative Justice: 'A Problem in Relationships' and 'A Duty of Active Kindness'

For William Morris Jones, then Professor of Politics at the London School of Economics, writing in 1949, the problem of bureaucracy in a democratic society lay in 'communication', in the need for an 'effective two-way conversation' so that 'the business of rule' is 'as little like a sermon or a lecture or a commanding officer's orders of the day as possible'. 'Talk', however, is not enough: there is an urgent need for 'ideas, techniques and devices too'. Those ideas, techniques and devices must, as far as Morris Jones is concerned, improve on the 'old channels of accountability and communication' and encourage us 'to feel our way towards new ones'. The success of this programme of revision will depend, however, not on their 'technical excellence' but on their 'acceptance by the citizen body' and their compatibility with 'the spirit of our institutions as a whole'. Critical to that venture, Morris Jones suggests, will be 'responsible and co-ordinated decentralisation', the removal of a sense of 'remoteness', and the 'rediscovery of the significant local community'. The 'problem of bureaucracy' is, in other words, at its core a 'problem in relationships', notably between 'official and public', state and citizen (Morris Jones 1949).

For Richard Crossman MP also, in his *Socialism and the New Despotism* (1956), the antidote to what he described as the 'age of oligopoly' lay in the exposure of 'irresponsible power' and challenge to the 'new managerial oligarchy' in both private and public sectors. Since, in his view, public authorities can also show 'managerialist tendencies, favour inequality and become a threat to freedom', the ambition should be to make 'those who control great concentrations of power fully accountable to the people' (Crossman 1956). As Leader of the House of Commons, Crossman, along with the then Lord Chancellor, Lord Gardiner, and future Cabinet Minister, Peter Shore, did much to encourage the 'ombudsman idea' in Britain and ensure the successful passage of the Parliamentary Commissioner Act in 1967 during Harold Wilson's premiership. Indeed, the Scandinavian 'ombudsman idea' was complementary to Crossman's enduring commitment to open government and accountability.

That Scandinavian provenance of the modern ombud institution (first developed in Sweden in 1809) was in keeping with the 'utopic discourse' of progress associated with the Nordic way of doing things in the post-war period, especially on the political left (Hilson 2008). Critical to this utopic discourse was the fundamental assertion that the state and individual share in the project of good citizenship and the creation of the good society. Any suggestion that the state is inherently antagonistic to individual freedom or well-being is largely discounted in favour of the view that the 'active' state has a positive obligation to enable individual and collective development. Insofar as the state is concerned with freedom, it is, to adapt Isaiah Berlin's distinction of positive and negative freedom, as much a question of creating positive 'freedom to' achieve human capability as policing negative 'freedom from' unwelcome state intrusion (Berlin 1969).

For Scandinavian social democrats, the developmental goal of the state should be increased awareness of mutual civic responsibility between state and citizen. It is from this tradition of Scandinavian 'civics' that the originally social democratic vision of the ombud institution emerged, the grievances of individual citizens serving the primary purpose of identifying 'sloppy or poorly thought through administrative action' without the need of an explicitly judicial process (O'Hara 2008: 116). In an interview in *The Listener* (12 May 1960), the then Danish Ombudsman, Professor Stefan Hurwitz, explained that the ombud was a democratic institution which could be traced back to the 'tribunes of the people' during the Roman Republic. As such, the ombud served, according to Hurwitz, as a 'safety valve to an old democracy', a means of acquiring a 'glimpse behind the scenes' of government and a 'bridge' between law and administration. The ombud was, he stated, a 'more ambiguous or amphibious institution' than either the judiciary or public administration, and one whose primary function was to investigate 'complaints or diseases in the body politic'.

This social democratic 'frame' of the relationship between citizen and state is therefore one of loyalty and co operation, the interests of citizens and the state being regarded as entirely compatible and capable of mutual reinforcement by the ombud institution. Any perceived conflict is to that extent mediated by a shared engagement in the public realm as the site of order, consensus and harmony. Furthermore, the ombud, and indeed administrative justice more generally, was to be regarded as an agent of the common good, or of public benefit, not just a vehicle of dispute resolution or individual redress. The Danish Ombudsman's discretion from the outset to embark on an investigation in the public interest, even without a specific complaint from an individual, further reinforced the separation of the ombud role from the form of reactive dispute resolution associated with the judicial process (Holm 1995: 19–20; Busck 1995).

An influential manifesto during this period, now almost forgotten, was Andrew Shonfield's *Modern Capitalism: the changing balance of public and private power* (1965). Shonfield argued that the challenge in ordering relationships between citizen and state was not that of 'designing a negative check on some bureaucratic vice' but of securing 'a positive effort of imagination and kindness from public officials in their treatment of private persons'. According to Shonfield, such effort was 'the characteristic mark of Scandinavian society', whilst its most familiar symbol was 'the Ombudsman'. In a 'would-be nomocracy' like Britain, with its 'overwhelming emphasis on legal procedure', the ombud institution would counter with a 'cult of bureaucratic humanity', in which the 'Ombudsman technique' would help sustain a more open style of public administration, not instead of administrative law but as a supplement to it, 'pushing the modern administration beyond mere justice, towards the recognition of a duty of active kindness in a society which grows increasingly dependent on the initiative and the sensibility of its public officials' (Shonfield 1965: 427).

Morris Jones' recognition that the 'problem of bureaucracy' is a 'problem in relationships' and Shonfield's advocacy of a 'duty of active kindness' provide potential routes to the reimagining of administrative justice. They do so in two ways in particular. First, they reinforce the importance of the 'relational self', rather than the isolated individual, as the primary agent in administrative justice and thereby of the 'relational rights' referred to earlier. Secondly, and consistently with that relational focus, they articulate the foundations of an ethic of care and 'active kindness' as the overriding institutional value of the democratic state that administrative justice must serve. The 'relational self' and the 'ethic of care' are to that extent key concepts that can be derived from the 'social democratic moment' and given new life in administrative justice reimagined 'as human rights in small places'.

* * *

The invocation of the social democratic moment and its values is integral to any contemporary reimagining of administrative justice and its institutional redesign. It is especially enlightening to glance back to that post-war period for a measure of historical perspective on the recent, rather more measured, configuration of administrative justice. A political and cultural consensus emerged then that stands in stark contrast to the neoliberal epoch which has largely prevailed in the UK since 1973, and from which the dominant mentalities of individualism, consumerism, and the New Public Management have derived much of their energy.

This chapter has re-evaluated administrative justice and human rights by reaffirming their intrinsic alliance, their necessary partnership, in the social democratic moment. As has been argued, that process of re-evaluation entails, however, the reinterpretation of administrative justice so that it is more determinedly set free from legalistic, consumerist and managerialist, expectations. Critically, such reinterpretation entails also a re-evaluation of the relationship of administrative justice with human rights in such a way that any lingering imbalance of rights talk in favour of individual civil rights is corrected by the reinstatement of the centrality of social rights and social citizenship. The next chapter considers the ways in which that intrinsic alliance has been undermined by the encroachment of neoliberal values on an originally shared social democratic vision.

References

Adler, M. (Ed.). (2010). *Administrative Justice in Context*. Oxford: Hart.

Adler, M. (2012). The Rise and Fall of Administrative Justice—A Cautionary Tale. *Socio-Legal Review, 8*, 29–54.

Ambedkar, B. R. (2010). Speech Delivered on 25 November 1949. In B. Das (Ed.), *Thus Spoke Ambedkar*. New Delhi: Navayana Publishing.

Ben Jelloun, T. (2016). *By Fire: Writings on the Arab Spring* (R. S. Nezami, Trans.). Evanston, IL: Northwestern University Press.

Berlin, I. (1969). Two Concepts of Liberty. In I. Berlin (Ed.), *Four Essays on Liberty*. Oxford: OUP.
Busck, L. (1995). The History and Development of the Institution of Ombudsman. In H. Gammeltoft-Hansen (Ed.), *The Danish Ombudsman*. Copenhagen: The Danish Ombudsman.
Cassin, R. (1972). *La Pensee et l'Action*. Boulogne: F Lalou.
Crossman, R. (1956). *Socialism and the New Despotism*. London: Fabian Society.
Equality and Human Rights Commission (EHRC). (2017). *Following Grenfell: The Human Rights and Equality Dimension. Statement from the Equality and Human Rights Commission.*
Feldman, D. (2010). Changes in Human Rights. In M. Adler (Ed.), *Administrative Justice in Context*. Oxford: Hart.
Gearty, C. (2006). *Can Human Rights Survive?* Cambridge: CUP.
Glendon, M. (2001). *A World Made New: Eleanor Roosevelt and the Universal Declaration of Human Rights*. New York: Random House.
Herring, J. (2017). Compassion, Ethics of Care and Legal Rights. *International Journal of Law in Context, 13*(2), 158–171.
Hilson. (2008). *The Nordic Model: Scandinavia since 1945*. Chicago: Chicago University Press.
Hirschman, A. O. (1970). *Exit, Voice and Loyalty: Responses to Decline in Firms, Organizations, and States*. Cambridge, MA: Harvard University Press.
Holm, N. E. (1995). The Ombudsman—A Gift from Scandinavia to the World. In H. Gammeltoft-Hansen (Ed.), *The Danish Ombudsman*. Copenhagen: The Danish Ombudsman.
Laverty, P., & Loach, K. (2016). *I, Daniel Blake*. Pontefract: Route Publishing.
Leggatt, S. A. (2001). *Tribunals for Users—One System, One Service*. London: Stationery Office.
Local Government and Social Care Ombudsman (LGSCO). (2018). *Annual Report 2017–18*. London: LGSCO.
Malik, C. (1968). Introduction. In O. Nolde (Ed.), *Free and Equal: Human Rights in Ecumenical Perspective*. Geneva: World Council of Churches.
Marshall, T. H. (1992). Citizenship and Social Class. In T. H. Marshall & T. Bottomore (Eds.), *Citizenship and Social Class*. London: Pluto.
Ministry of Justice. (2017). Tribunals and Gender Recognition Certificate Statistics Quarterly July–September 2017.
Ministry of Justice. (2018). Tribunals and Gender Recognition Certificate Statistics Quarterly April–June 2018.
Morris Jones, W. H. (1949). *Socialism and Bureaucracy*. London: Fabian Society.
Mullen, T. (2017). Access to Justice in Administrative Law and Administrative Justice. In E. Palmer et al. (Eds.), *Austerity and Access to Justice*. London: Bloomsbury.
Nason, S. (2018). *Administrative Justice: Wales' First Devolved Justice System: Evaluation and Recommendations*. Bangor University.

Newton, L. (2010). *House of Lords Hansard*, 29 November 2010, Col. 1325.
O'Cinneide, C. (2018). The Social Security (Scotland) Act 2018—A Rights-Based Approach to Social Security? *Edinburgh Law Review, 23*, 123–130.
O'Hara, G. (2008). The Intellectuals' Ideal: British Views of Scandinavia in the 1950s and 1960s. In J. E. Myhre (Ed.), *Intellectuals in the Public Sphere in Britain and Norway after World War II*. Oslo: Oslo Academic Press.
Parliamentary and Health Service Ombudsman (PHSO). (2018). *Annual Report 2017–18*.
Roosevelt, E. (1948). The Promise of Human Rights. *Foreign Affairs*. In A. Black (Ed.), *Courage in a Dangerous World: The Political Writings of Eleanor Roosevelt* (pp. 156–168). New York: Columbia University Press.
Roosevelt, E. (1958). *The Great Question*. Remarks delivered at the United Nations. New York: United Nations.
Roosevelt, E. (2016). *The Moral Basis of Democracy*. New York: Open Road.
Shonfield, A. (1965). *Modern Capitalism: The Changing Balance of Public and Private Power*. London: OUP.
Sunstein, C. (2004). *The Second Bill of Rights: FDR's Unfinished Revolution and Why We Need It More Than Ever*. New York: Basic Books.
Thomas, R. (2011). *Speech to the Administrative Justice and Tribunals Council Annual Conference*, 17 November 2011. Administrative Justice and Tribunals Council.
Thomas, R., & Tomlinson, J. (2017). Mapping Current Issues in Administrative Justice: Austerity and the 'More Bureaucratic Rationality' Approach. *Journal of Social Welfare and Family Law, 39*(3), 380–399.
UK Administrative Justice Institute (UKAJI). (2018). *A Research Roadmap for Administrative Justice*. Colchester: University of Essex.
White Paper: *Transforming Public Services: Complaints, Redress and Tribunals*. (2004). London: Department for Constitutional Affairs.

CHAPTER 3

A Neoliberal Eclipse

Abstract This chapter examines the erosion of the social democratic foundations of administrative justice and human rights by a form of neo-liberalism that prioritises individualism, market values and 'business as usual'. The chapter highlights the dominance in human rights discourse of libertarian civil rights at the expense of relational social rights and the encroachment of the common law mentality on extra-judicial forms of administrative justice. It concludes that the prevailing framework for interpreting both administrative justice and human rights is shaped by the values of the individual 'user', 'system' and 'closure' to such an extent that there appears no alternative path available to either.

Keywords Legalism • Individualism • User • System • Closure

Human Rights and Law's Empire

Fundamental to the preservation of the separation of civil rights from social rights has been the part assigned to 'law' in the promotion and protection of human rights. The enlargement of law's empire has established, in effect, a two-tier system which recognises civil and political rights as superior, with legal enforceability the essential criterion of credibility. As a result, the desirability of creating 'constitutional' social rights has become the subject of protracted debate, and the 'transformation' of human rights

M. Doyle, N. O'Brien, *Reimagining Administrative Justice*,
https://doi.org/10.1007/978-3-030-21388-6_3

seen to be dependent on the accommodation by courts, not just in India or South Africa, of practices that might make the justiciability of social rights compatible with democratic politics (Gearty and Mantouvlou 2011; Fredman 2011; King 2012).

Countering this subordination of social rights is a task taken up by Professor Paul Hunt, former UN Special Rapporteur on the Right to Health, when he signals the need to argue from basics for the very inclusion of social rights in the human rights 'system' (Hunt 2017). In his foreword to Hunt's *Social Rights are Human Rights*, journalist Paul Mason cited the *Platforma de Afectados por la Hipoteca*, a social movement for the right to housing in Spain, as:

> *just one example of the way social justice movements are using the internationally protected and formally stated social rights to legitimise resistance [to injustice], such as rights to an adequate standard of living, affordable housing, accessible education, an equitable health system, and social security based on respect, not sanctions.* (Hunt 2017: 5)

Meanwhile, Hunt argues, in the UK the human rights 'system' is effectively 'rigged', in the sense that 'it privileges civil and political rights and neglects social rights' which are 'emancipatory and position us all as rights holders, not service users'. Yet, importantly, 'Social rights are not the preserve of lawyers and other technocrats. They are not just about going to court. Explicit social rights have the power to dignify and emancipate individuals and communities. They can shape policies and practice' (Hunt 2017: 7–8).

The emancipatory power of social rights in respect not just of 'individuals' but of 'communities' invites reflection on the need, even in the sphere of social rights entitlement, to transcend any lingering individualism and emphasis on legal enforcement in their realisation. The Universal Declaration can, and should, be read as part of the response to pre-war social need and post-war social reconstruction, not just as a charter of individual libertarian values. To that extent, the human rights vision can be seen as part of that broader movement for social citizenship that characterised the post-war welfare state (Marshall 1992; Bottomore 1992). As human rights historian Samuel Moyn has argued forcefully (Moyn 2018), even the advocacy of individualised social rights is a poor substitute for meaningful social citizenship and equality. The pursuit of a 'social minimum', or of 'subsistence rights', is, as he emphasises, a demonstrably unsuccessful route to material equality and participation.

Furthermore, the primary 'social citizenship' focus of administrative justice on the relationship between citizen and state has the potential, through its re-alliance with the originally ambitious conception of social rights, to transcend the individualism of libertarian civil rights entitlement. In this way, administrative justice can serve to reconfigure social rights advocacy itself so that it preserves the egalitarian thrust of social citizenship and serves a more radical objective than that of individual liberty, even when buttressed by individual subsistence rights. The trajectory of human rights itself has, however, made such an alliance difficult to achieve.

The Individualistic Trajectory of Human Rights

As argued in the previous chapter, like administrative justice, human rights can be seen to have emerged from a broader project of social reconstruction that recognised the importance of the public realm and the individual person conceived as fundamentally relational, inextricably bound up with the shared interest of other people and the common good. For the advocates of the Universal Declaration, it was the cultural force of human rights as a network of values that gave it weight rather than its enforceability as a legal code.

In the intervening years, that broad vision has largely ceded ground to a much narrower and legalistic conception of human rights that sees legal enforceability as the glittering prize of human rights advocacy. The emphasis on the individual as the bearer of rights has been a central feature of that evolution and, as Moyn argues, a means by which human rights has inadvertently become the prop of neoliberal values. Far from human rights being a vehicle for social citizenship and equality, they have become the harbingers of individual liberty and of property, privacy and profit.

Such individualism reinforces the view of human rights as a struggle between competing interests that is best resolved by adversarial litigation. The inherent drama of adversarialism lends itself to the impression that there is something essentially dramatic and agonistic about human rights discourse, that human rights typically concern themselves with extraordinary situations and unusual (often unusually bad) individuals rather than ordinary situations and (usually decent) communities trying to share a life in common. These libertarian civil rights seek resolution in the court process, both domestic and international, and capture the headlines. In the meantime, social rights, typically subject to more deliberative mediation out of the court setting, are perceived as inferior and in need of a strategy to achieve a measure of legal enforcement if they are to have credibility (Fredman 2011; Gearty and Mantouvlou 2011; King 2012).

In the UK, for example, it is telling that by far the best known human rights NGO is Liberty, the former National Council for Civil Liberties. In the period following 9/11 and the London terrorist attacks in July 2005, Liberty became especially prominent in the debates about the treatment of suspected terrorists, asylum seekers and convicted criminals. This exclusive association of human rights with issues of war and peace, and crime and punishment, led to belated attempts to reclaim human rights for the ordinary and day-to-day, to 'bring human rights home' (Halliday and Schmidt 2004; Klug 2000). In recognition of the original policy intention to create a 'human rights culture' with the introduction of the Human Rights Act 1998, organisations such as the British Institute of Human Rights, and later the Equality and Human Rights Commission, began a programme of work to encourage the view that human rights are the concern of ordinary citizens in their day-to-day transactions with health services, social services, schools and housing authorities. Alongside were initiatives, jointly with the Ministry of Justice, to encourage regulators, inspectorates and ombuds to find resonance in human rights principles, rather than human rights law, for their work outside the formal legal setting of the courtroom (Equality and Human Rights Commission 2008, 2014).

Such moves were in effect an acknowledgement that the international human rights 'system', including the accreditation apparatus overseen by the UN, had become too preoccupied with legal powers and legal enforcement, with the result that National Human Rights Institutions (NHRIs), with their systematic approach to protection and promotion, were incapable of embedding the changes in mentality needed for a truly human rights culture. In Europe, where the Council of Europe's civil rights charter, the European Convention on Human Rights, is enforced by the Strasbourg Court but the Social Charter is overseen by the more collaborative and deliberative Committee of Social Rights, the then Human Rights Commissioner, Thomas Hammarberg, made it a priority to encourage ombud institutions throughout Europe to see themselves as part of the national human rights 'structure' and so enable the realisation of human rights values through networks, such as that of the European Ombudsman's Network of Ombudsmen, rather than through the UN-sanctioned system of human rights enforcement (Hammarberg 2007a, b).

Such initiatives represented a departure from the legalistic ambition of dispute resolution and closure in preference for a more deliberative and iterative pursuit of changes of mind and heart, for a prospective outlook instead of a resolutely retrospective and remedial approach. They reflect also the recognition that rights are better understood in terms of relationships than in the assertion of individual entitlement. Those, for example, who advocate compassion and an ethic of care as the scaffolding of progressive law find in relational rights the tools needed to enable caring relationships and responsibilities, and so promote more relational values (Herring 2017: 165). Yet despite such aspirations, the dominant motif, both in the UK and internationally, has been the spectre of the courtroom as the primary theatre for the enactment of individualised, adversarial and libertarian human rights drama. For the most part, the advocates of equality and relational rights have had to look elsewhere for the realisation of their ideals.

In the light of the trajectory described above, it can be seen that the original and social democratic alliance of human rights with the active state has been undermined by an encroaching legalism that has prioritised individual entitlement and legal closure as its trademark characteristics. As Moyn remarks, 'The Universal Declaration…is best understood as canonizing political and social rights as part of a consensus that citizens required new and powerful states at home' (Moyn 2018: 7). On this account, social rights were quite simply 'part of a larger egalitarian package', a reimagining of nineteenth-century liberalism's urgent protection of individual rights in the form of 'freedom of contract and the person and the sanctity of property and transaction' (Moyn 2018: 6). As Moyn adds, 'the companionship between human rights and market fundamentalism was not inevitable' (Moyn 2018: 8). Instead it was the coalition of 'ethically individualist grounds' and the extrication of human rights from their 'welfare state crucible' that made human rights 'hostages' of neoliberalism and of a global but 'individualist project' (Moyn 2018: 8). The move from culture to law, from state to individual, has helped facilitate that process, and with it the impoverishment of human rights as a sustainable and democratic ethic for life in small places.

Administrative Justice in the Shadow of the Law

As with social rights, and as argued in the previous chapter, the original policy ambition for administrative justice in the post-war period was also explicitly for non-legalistic, or extra-legal, design, so that tribunals, public inquiries, and ombuds would sit outside the traditional judicial and court structure. Indeed, it was that extra-judicial character of administrative justice that fuelled suspicion that this nascent 'process pluralism' constituted a threat to the common law and posed a challenge to the Rule of Law as narrowly conceived by constitutional lawyer A.V. Dicey at the end of the nineteenth century. The post-war social democratic moment offered a fertile environment for this extra-legal conception of administrative justice.

Notwithstanding the extra-legal aspirations for post-war administrative justice, the design of our current approaches to administrative justice is nevertheless emphatically shaped by our local understanding of law and of what it entails, in other words by our 'legal consciousness' (Creutzfeldt 2018). In the context of England and Wales, that is an understanding in which the common law and its associated sets of assumptions and priorities, its mentality, loom large. The common law mentality crucially directed the translation of administrative justice as a political vision of the relationship between the individual and the state into something much narrower; the adoption in public law of the language of 'dispute resolution' has contributed to this narrowed conception. The institutional forms achieved by that translation as a result came to resemble more and more the court system from which they were at first expected to stand apart.

Jurisprudential suspicions of administrative justice already had a substantial pedigree in Britain. In particular, Dicey's celebration of the Rule of Law, and his dismay at the activities of the *Conseil d'Etat* and the development of the *droit administratif* in France, formed many generations of Anglophone lawyers who came to share a set of basic assumptions. The idea that the executive and state officials might somehow evade the reach of the courts through the establishment of alternative institutional structures was anathema. Lord Chief Justice Hewart's *The New Despotism* (1929) constituted a tirade against the very notion of administrative justice as anything other than the subordination of public administration to the settled boundaries and full rigour of the common law.

Chief among the assumptions underpinning the common law mentality and reverence for a narrow conception of the Rule of Law was the assertion that the law, despite appearances, is in fact an 'internally coherent and unified body of rules', capable of coherent interpretation by paying careful attention to the cumulative pronouncements of the judges (Sugarman 1986: 27). More importantly, however, such a mentality conveyed a strong political message: that the law (primarily through case law) and the legal profession (centrally, the judiciary) play a major role in protecting individual freedom, so that 'the form as well as the content of the law becomes imbricated within, and synonymous with, our very definition of individual freedom and liberty, and thereby acquires an additional patina of reverence and universality' (Sugarman 1986). Insofar as such a mentality had room for human rights, for example, it was for a distinctly individualistic and libertarian model of civil rights. Indeed, the common law mentality, with its strong attachment to a rigorously individualistic brand of libertarianism, sat well with the aspiration to impose effective constraints on collective and state power and so protect the 'little man' (sic) from the state's apparently relentless intrusion.

Yet the tendency for such celebration of the Rule of Law to confine rights-talk to negative prohibition on the state is strong. In the words of American jurist Morton Horwitz, whilst the idea of the Rule of Law has 'undoubtedly restrained power' it also 'prevents power's benevolent exercise. It creates formal equality—a not inconsiderable virtue—but it promotes substantive inequality by creating a consciousness that radically separates law from politics, means from ends, processes from outcomes. By promoting procedural justice it enables the shrewd, the calculating, and the wealthy to manipulate its forms to their own advantage. And it satisfies and legitimates an adversarial, competitive and atomistic conception of human relations' (Horwitz 1977: 566). It does not, in other words, have much time for social rights, social citizenship, or for recognition of the 'relational' dimension of ordinary human life.

The idea that law takes place exclusively in the courts has important repercussions for administrative justice. Other potentially relevant institutions such as tribunals, ombuds, mediation and public inquiries are liable to easy marginalisation or, alternatively, colonisation by the legalist mentality. In short, 'legal constitutionalism focuses almost exclusively on public law as it is developed and enforced in the courts, such focus in effect amounting to little more than the application of the common law mind to the field of public law' (Tomkins 2005: 15).

The implications of this common law mentality were identified in one striking and particular form by Richard Titmuss in 1971. Titmuss, one of the architects of the welfare state in Britain, was by then a member of the Supplementary Benefits Commission. His particular concern was what he saw as the encroachment of legalism on the exercise of administrative discretion. Such encroachment he identified as the policy of the New Diceyists, 'a movement that has emerged in recent years in unexpected and strange disguises in Britain and the United States'. One notably strange disguise, he suggested, was that of the welfare rights movement, which had been imported to Britain from the USA. Whereas it was understandable, thought Titmuss, that the political right should be enamoured of Dicey's abhorrence of the power of unelected officials and 'tribunals composed of lay people', more surprising was the willingness of progressives on the left uncritically to support the demand for 'income-maintenance rights, judicialised appeal systems and equality of access to material facts contained in files or office procedure books'.

In Titmuss' view, this 'organised, militant "consumerism"' and associated fear of all bureaucracy was misplaced, since the actively benevolent state was unthinkable without some form of bureaucratic power. The US solution of advocating more lawyers, legal precedent and case law was a false one: 'It is assumed that justice will be advanced if case law is substituted for administrative decision; if all appeal systems are judicialised and claimants are represented by lawyers; if all discretionary cash additions are abolished; if access to the courts is made available to all claimants; and if the adversary system replaces the inquisitorial lay tribunal' (Titmuss 1971: 118).

Drawing on the socio-legal work of Phillipe Nonet, Titmuss challenged the assumption that 'claimants as a whole', as opposed to 'just one lone claimant', benefited from such legalistic approaches. According to Nonet's research, the more 'legal' hearings became, so 'the aims of health and rehabilitation progress were increasingly frustrated by case law, legal mystification and a litigious courthouse atmosphere'. In short, for Titmuss the fundamental problem rested in 'the pathology of legalism' (Titmuss 1971: 124) and in 'legal imprisonment in precedence and the cumbrous process of gladiatorial combat' (Titmuss 1971: 129).

Traces of this New Diceyism identified by Titmuss can be detected among the active promoters of administrative justice in the 1950s and 60s, and so provided the foundation for the judicialisation of administrative justice that Titmuss lamented. The most influential collective force for the promotion of administrative justice during this period was the campaigning body Justice, established in 1957 as the British section of the International Commission of Jurists (ICJ) at The Hague. The ICJ's stated objective was 'to seek to foster understanding of and respect for the Rule of Law'. In similar spirit, the stated objective of Justice in its constitution was 'to uphold and strengthen the principles of the Rule of Law in the territories for which the British Parliament is directly or indirectly responsible; in particular to assist in the maintenance of the highest standards of the administration of justice and in the protection of the fundamental liberties of the individual' (Stacey 1971: 10–14).

To that extent, Justice can be seen as strongly affiliated to Dicey's prescription of the Rule of Law and individual civil liberties, and to the common law mind which such an outlook helped to consolidate. Frank Stacey, in his 1971 book *The British Ombudsman*, tellingly describes the tiled mural then in Justice's offices off Fleet Street: on the left there is a prison, and in front of it a huge, driverless bulldozer pursuing naked men, women and children, who in turn run towards a bearded figure supported by a kneeling angel. As Stacey explains, 'The prison and the bulldozer represent the unfeeling machinery of the modern state which (in the words of Justice's own description of the mural) is "threatening to crush and engulf the common man (sic), who is fleeing to a Mosaic figure upholding Justice and administering it with Mercy"' (Stacey 1971: 14).

It was Justice which in 1961 promoted the ombud as the key development in administrative justice, with the publication of the Whyatt Report. By the time the Wilson government finally gave legislative form, with the Parliamentary Commissioner Act 1967, to 'the Ombudsman idea' and its policy ambition of 'humanising the whole administration of the state' (Labour Party 1964: 24), the common law mentality had already infused its future institutional design. As historian Glen O'Hara has observed, 'It was the impetus given by Justice to the creation of a constitutional and legal office that helped give the office of Ombudsman just that character' (O'Hara 2012: 100). Any aspiration towards informality or towards using the ombud to shape the state in what Shonfield had called a 'cult of bureaucratic humanity' was to that extent impaired by this legalistic turn. Instead the 'nomocracy' to which Shonfield had alluded as typical of the British way was well-placed to tighten its grip.

The Shadows Deepen: The 2004 White Paper

That process continued apace in the wake of the Leggatt Report in 2001, albeit in alliance with the principles of the New Public Management ('efficiency, effectiveness and economy'), with a strong emphasis on the priority of the individual 'user' of the tribunal 'system' and with a predilection for 'proportionate dispute resolution' as the preferred route to effective closure for the individual (Drewry 2009). The Tribunals, Courts and Enforcement Act 2007 took the process a step further, with the creation of the Administrative Justice and Tribunals Council (AJTC) to replace Franks' Council on Tribunals and to oversee not just tribunals but ombuds and all administrative decision-making. At the same time the creation of an integrated courts and tribunals service, separate tribunal 'chambers', tribunal 'judges' and an Upper Tribunal served to bring the tribunals ever closer to the courts. As Drewry concluded in 2009, 'Recent reforms have carried forward an evolutionary tendency to systematise and judicialise the structure and working of tribunals' (Drewry 2009: 57).

The template for the 2007 Act and the primary source for identifying the texture of contemporary administrative justice is the preceding White Paper, *Transforming Public Services: Complaints, Redress and Tribunals* (2004). The White Paper was one of the UK government's most ambitious redesign initiatives, its aim to bring together a disparate collection of tribunal institutions into one coherent organisation and to reform the delivery of public services. Its design proposals were to be 'tested by a simple criterion: what is best for the users?' Arising out of the Leggatt Review, which identified tribunals as an incoherent set of institutions and not at all a 'system' in any sense, the White Paper broadened its scope to include the wider administrative justice landscape and sought to 'systematise' that 'landscape' by identifying essential design features, the key component being 'proportionality'. The aim of this new tribunals service would 'not be just to process cases according to law…[but] to help to prevent and resolve disputes, using any appropriate method' (White Paper 2004: 5). The ambition was explicitly 'to develop a range of policies and services that, so far as possible, will help people to avoid problems and legal disputes in the first place: and, where they cannot, provide tailored solutions to resolve the dispute as quickly and cost-effectively as possible. It can be summed up as "Proportionate Dispute Resolution"' (White Paper 2004).

The focus of the White Paper was therefore the individual user. Its reformist agenda was laudable enough: to upend the traditional focus on courts and the judiciary and instead start with real-world problems that ordinary people face. However, in so doing, it placed individual 'choice' and 'empowerment' at the centre. It spoke of 'nipping problems in the bud' (through advice and information to get problems resolved early) and of a 'tailored dispute resolution service' to be used when that 'nipping' was unsuccessful. It explained that 'what people want' entails a range of potentially competing 'factors', including speed, cost, privacy, simplicity, rigour, finality, and participation. Revealingly, the White Paper characterised the fragmented approach to citizen grievances as resembling that of a travel agent insisting 'on knowing whether you want to go by aeroplane, train or ferry before asking what your destination is' (White Paper 2004:

9). In doing so, the White Paper betrayed its intention to present users as 'consumers' of public services and of administrative justice, with all the valorisation of 'choice' and 'customer service' that goes with a consumer-driven approach, and set its task as that of finding ways of 'combining the strengths of all the redress methods so as to give people real choice and a genuinely responsive service, equal to the best service delivery organisations' (White Paper 2004: 9).

This appetite for consumerism and individual 'dispute resolution' and for ensuring the best chance of optimal 'service delivery' has subsequently become manifest in the emphasis on identifying individual cases that are suitable for 'proportionate resolution' out of court. From the outset, and during its short existence, the AJTC was the institutional guardian of the White Paper's integrated vision; its remit was to keep under review 'the administrative justice system as a whole with a view to making it accessible, fair and efficient' and to ensure that 'the relationships between the courts, tribunals and ombudsmen and alternative dispute resolution providers satisfactorily reflect the needs of users' (AJTC 2010). The AJTC's concerns with 'relationships' did not, notably, extend beyond the 'dispute resolution' system to encompass the earlier aspiration of actively shaping the relationship between citizen and state. It is significant that when the AJTC asked, in its 2012 paper *Putting It Right*, how to match grievance with redress ('which horses for which courses?'), it did so in the same language of proportionate dispute resolution used in the White Paper, putting forward a list of 'mapping factors' to help inform decisions about which redress route was appropriate for which grievance and to inform the design of redress.

Such mapping factors or checklists by their very nature tend not to take account of the variability and unpredictability of human behaviour; they rely on 'objective' factors such as claim value, the cost of pursuing litigation, or an abstract notion of the public interest. Rarely do they reflect sufficiently the fact that individuals make choices about addressing grievances based on their own circumstances, fears, hopes and idiosyncrasies. Of greater concern is that checklists, as navigating tools, presume that proportionality is the key shared destination—that there is consensus on there being 'too much Rolls and not enough Mini' in our justice system, as Harry Street said in his 1968 Hamlyn Lecture, *Justice in the Welfare State* (Street 1975). Proportionality has maintained a firm grip on administrative justice design, yet it warrants challenge as an underpinning value governing the relationship between citizen and state. Proportionality betrays a narrow view of whom administrative justice is 'for', prioritising individual users rather than the community of users, while at the same time assuming that user needs are predictable and fixed; it begs the question of who assesses proportionality and from what perspective; and it prioritises closure as an ideal value—getting to the end in the most efficient way, and returning to business as usual, at the expense of any shared public value.

The implicit frame of the White Paper proposal is the desirability of 'system', of a well-oiled machine where the parts cohere, of explicit concern for the interests of the individual 'user' and of the achievement of dispute resolution or effective 'closure'. The AJTC shared that 'user focus' as the core principle of its oversight of administrative justice, which more decisively than before was now conceived as a coherent 'system' to rival the better established criminal and civil justice systems, with the notion of proportionate dispute resolution as the underlying value. In these ways, the contemporary design of administrative justice betrays its absorption within a legalistic mentality, where the values of the common law, its individualism, its boundaries, and its libertarianism constrain the options for more expansive reimagining.

Administrative Justice Orthodoxies Under Fire

The contemporary regime has not, however, been without valuable critique which can help identify a way forward, not least by its more self-conscious attention to the necessity of deliberate 'design'. For example, the emphasis on user focus as both 'key value' and 'aspirational normative standard' (Tomlinson 2017) has, perhaps ironically, attracted the sceptical attention of the Supreme Court, which in its decision on the Unison challenge on tribunal fees in 2017 vigorously objected to the prevailing assumption in government that those who use the 'justice system' can reasonably be categorised as 'consumers':

> *At the heart of Lord Reed's critique of the government is that, in their assessment of whether tribunals fees were a good idea, it focused too much on users as consumers of legal services and did not focus enough on the wider role that a user may play as a citizen in the maintenance of a good political community.* (Tomlinson 2017: 532)

Indeed, as Tomlinson suggests, the term 'user focus' is fraught with difficulty. Noting that the UK Government prioritises 'user focus' and that it 'could be said to now be a key value of administrative justice', he suggests there is an underlying disagreement coming to the surface (Tomlinson 2017: 530). Which users, and what about potential users who could but decline to (or are unable to) use the 'system', and those other people who are in some sense 'users'—decision-makers within government, complaint handlers within ombud schemes, advisers, advocates and legal representatives, the judiciary? Tomlinson argues for distinguishing between the two senses of user-friendliness—the 'consumerist' sense, in which justice is a product to be purchased and consumed, and the 'accessibility' sense, prioritising convenience and accessibility to users. There is a third aspect of 'user' that has particular relevance for administrative justice—the public interest of a community of users, in its widest sense—and it may be that the emerging hold that design thinking has taken on administrative justice indicates a shift towards a new conception of 'user focus', encompassing all three senses, and towards a more holistic, less legalistic design approach (Sossin 2017).

In their study of design principles in administrative justice, Bondy and Le Sueur (2012) interrogate but ultimately accept the principles of 'user focus' and proportionality, and indeed one of their proposed principles is that mechanisms for redress 'should ensure value for money and proportionality'. Their study coincided with the AJTC's work on mapping the administrative justice landscape, and both projects effectively endorse the White Paper's valorisation of proportionality and user focus as appropriate aims. Despite this, Bondy and Le Sueur identify a number of challenges in applying this principle to design (or re-design) of 'pathways' of redress. These include the difficulty of quantifying costs, the tension between efficiency and quality, and the need to assess the costs of unresolved disputes and unmet need, which includes the impact 'on individuals and society in terms of physical and mental health, solvency, education, crime and self-esteem' (Bondy and Le Sueur 2012: 51). Key is the challenge of identifying from whose perspective the assessment of proportionality is made (operator, funder, user?). These perspectives offer up a different 'formula' for such assessment: 'unit cost' versus claim value (which they note is not readily quantifiable in administrative justice), and 'deserving' versus 'undeserving', in which resources are rationed and the trivial and vexatious complaints are filtered out. They argue that what is often not factored into the proportionality equation are lesson learning and the dissemination of good practice.

In identifying the 'drivers for design' of administrative redress mechanisms, Bondy and Le Sueur resign themselves to the fact that it is 'the operators' (i.e. those who work within the 'system') who have decisively shaped the design of redress mechanisms, not the users, and definitely not the users in a participatory way. Despite much talk of 'user-led design', in fact most administrative justice design since the 1990s has been couched in the language of 'consumer journey', 'customer satisfaction' and 'efficiency'. This is language that reflects the shift to New Public Management principles and the growth of a managerial and consumerist focus in administrative justice (Adler 2010; Gill et al. 2019), both of which impose on administrative justice 'agendas whose philosophical underpinnings ... fundamentally jar with the provision of justice' (Gill et al. 2019).

The orthodoxy that administrative justice is, or should be, a coherent system also comes under scrutiny in Bondy and Le Sueuer's analysis of design principles. They propose that the 'organic administrative justice landscape' may well have advantages over a 'more tightly controlled system' in that it facilitates changes and allows for innovation (Bondy and Le Sueur 2012: 33). Their four redress models—supervisory, overlapping jurisdiction (about the relationship between redress mechanisms and government agencies) and filter and resolution (two features of redress mechanisms) perhaps cast doubt on the idea of a bounded system. Overlapping jurisdiction—between, for example, the public-sector ombud and the Administrative Court—illustrates the illusion of the original design intention of 'system', as the legislation establishing both the Parliamentary Commissioner and the Local Government Ombudsman stipulated that neither would have jurisdiction over cases that could be routed to the Administrative Court, a tribunal, or other legal proceedings. That 'statutory bar' is now, in practice, increasingly permeable, suggesting there is appetite to move from hard boundaries within a 'system' to seams in a more open fabric.

Whilst critiques of the 2004 White Paper approach provide a potential check on the prevailing 'legalism' of the underlying mentality, they serve to highlight the extent to which even attempts at reform in the field of administrative justice have been constrained by the motifs of individual user, system and closure imported from the court-based culture of the common law. Writing in 2012, Michael Adler (Adler 2012) reflected on the real differences in culture between courts and tribunals and on the little room for doubt about 'who the senior partner is' in the merger achieved by the unified Courts and Tribunals Service. There is, he concluded, 'real danger that a "court culture" will prevail' and that 'the distinctive approach to dispute resolution that has been associated with tribunals, and championed by its supporters, will be put at risk' (Adler 2012: 46).

More recent administrative justice scholarship has reinforced the view that the dominance of legalism in administrative justice is misplaced. It has been noted, for example, that a form of legal consciousness that gives special weight to distinctively legal norms simply creates false expectations of public interest ombuds, even when, or perhaps especially when, they in fact aspire to extra-legal values (Creutzfeldt 2018). Frontline public officials, by contrast, frequently take matters into their own hands and make a 'bureaucratic retreat' from the rigorous application of jurisprudential norms (Hertogh 2018). As a result, the 'new administrative justice' is at least in part, and increasingly, marked in practice by a style of 'responsive legality' that, like responsive or reflexive regulation more generally, is more fluid and flexible than earlier more 'repressive' or 'autonomous' forms of legality (Richards 2019; Nonet and Selznick 1978). Nevertheless, there is still need for more embedding of humane values and basic human rights principles in the work of street-level bureaucrats, for example in UK welfare benefit agencies (Adler 2018), and for more cultivation of humane 'dispositions', not just efficient and effective decision-making, on the front-line (Zacka 2017). To that extent, the prevailing mood is one of increased scepticism about the ability of administrative justice to operate democratically and humanely whilst adhering to a legalistic mentality and its values of individual user perspective, system and resolution.

The Pathology of Legalism

The expansive ambitions of post-war law reform can to that extent be seen to have foundered on the rock of what Titmuss had called in 1971 the 'pathology of legalism'. Insofar as administrative justice can be said to have been subjected to any consistent principles of design, those principles reflect the common law mentality. The merits of such a mentality, in terms of the protection of individual liberty, adversarial testing of evidence, the promulgation of legal precedent, and the standardisation of legal process are not negligible, and indeed cherished by some (and not just 'litigation romanticists') (Mulcahy 2013). Nevertheless, its emergence as the abiding ethos and default position in administrative justice represents a significant constraint on the original aspiration towards extra-legal design. Instead, the model of judicial review, notwithstanding the decline in the number of successful applications for permission since the Bowman reforms in 2000 and evidence of high settlement rates (Bondy and Sunkin 2009; Bondy et al. 2015), retains its allure as a benchmark of legitimate expectation.

Although research suggests that claimants gain a range of tangible benefits from judicial review, especially when they have legal representation, and court judgments have a significant impact in relation to policy, procedure, the clarity of the law and civil rights protection (Bondy et al. 2015), to elevate the judicial review process to that of model for other parts of the administrative justice system impoverishes the range and depth of approaches available, especially as a vehicle for promoting relational values and social citizenship. It is perhaps notable in this regard that the use of mediation in judicial review proceedings remains low, despite findings (albeit from limited application in this context) that it is a potentially valuable complement to judicial determination (Bondy et al. 2009; Bondy and Doyle 2011).

Such observations on the drift of administrative justice into models of design shaped by the values of the common law mentality might be of merely antiquarian interest if contemporary design aspirations were significantly different and free from the imaginative constraints of legalism. Recent reforms have pushed administrative justice further down the route of judicialisation, however. The suggestion that public sector ombuds should acquire 'own initiative' powers independently of any 'individual cause of action' or complaint, for example, has caused dismay in Whitehall. Meanwhile, the ombuds are held accountable against a template that in essence is that of the common law courts, with commentators and users lamenting their inability to mimic more closely the judicial process with its individualism, systematic aspirations and prospect of closure by way of something as near as possible to an adversarial hearing of both sides.

More generally, as Conor Gearty has demonstrated, there has been an outbreak of what he calls 'common law revivalism', and not merely as a weapon with which to pierce the Human Rights Act 1998. The marks of this revivalism are the tendency of even liberal judges to assert that everything in the Human Rights Act was already inherent in the common law, that law (not Parliament) is sovereign and the perennial source of ancient English liberties, and that the courts have as their sole task the adjudication of individual disputes, the parties pitched in adversarial combat, with no place for interventions or public interest argument (Gearty 2016).

There stands in the Royal Courts of Justice on the Strand a visual image to match this vision: it is of a judge, sculpted in stone, sword in hand, armour in place, muscles rippling in defence of the common law (as Gearty notes, there is not much room for the feminine in the standard image of the common law). Whilst rightly congratulated on its defence of the liberty of the individual (or at least of some individuals—as Geary remarks, the common law is generally against mob rule unless the mob is 'our mob'), the common law 'has not been so good at recognising any kind of deeper structure to the society out of which arise the disputes that its judges encounter…it is blind to power and privilege and therefore to the commitments to equality and non-discrimination with which those discontented with the status quo seek to achieve change. Historically these ideas have had to fight the common law, not rely on it' (Gearty 2016: 23).

The design of administrative justice in practice has been shaped by the common law mind or, more pejoratively, the pathology of legalism. The political drivers for change in the post-war social democratic moment, notwithstanding their inherent tensions, have been lost in the translation into institutional and 'quasi-legal' practice of that original political impulse. The individual 'user', the ideal of efficient 'system', and the ambition of dispute resolution or 'closure' achieved by a one-off encounter with formal adjudication persist as the ideal design features. A narrow view of the rule of law and the rigours of the common law mentality still largely prevail.

'User', 'System' and 'Closure': The End of History?

Human rights and administrative justice can be seen to share common origins in the post-war social democratic moment. As a result, their natural habitat is extra-legal and rooted in the ambitions of a broadly democratic culture, a redefinition of the relationship between citizen and state, and between citizen and citizen. As such they share also in the values of social citizenship, humane administration and a duty of active kindness. Their provenance is the everyday and the ordinary.

Yet in accordance with a similar trajectory, they have been colonised by law's empire and dislodged from their proper place in the political sphere. Through a steady process of incremental erosion both administrative justice and human rights have become complicit with a different world view, with the values of the marketplace, consumerism, individualism and the New Public Management. They have unwittingly become the agents of that neoliberalism that has stalked the public realm since the 1970s and hollowed out the common good. So pervasive has this corrosive process been that the dominant values of individual, system and closure appear unassailable. Modern human rights, like modern administrative justice, seem inseparable from individual choice, efficient management and business as usual. In such a context, democratic value is reduced to periodic plebiscite and freedom from state intrusion, as far as compatible with a crudely utilitarian metric. Whilst there is scope for tinkering with the mechanics, the essentials lie beyond reproach and alternative narratives banished to the realm of fantasy. For human rights and administrative justice, the end of history can be safely announced.

* * *

That might have been the conclusion until not so long ago, until the financial crash of 2008 cast doubt on the viability of the regulatory regimes that had prevailed since the 1980s and in 2016 the election of Donald Trump as President of the USA and the referendum on Brexit in the UK made fragile the established liberal democratic order. Populism, whether of the political left or right, invites a reassessment of the relationship between citizen and state, between the private and the public realms. Human rights and administrative justice, so closely implicated in that relationship, in turn find themselves exposed to the cross-currents of a new history and new forms of social movement.

This moment of crisis they share with the public culture more broadly. Belatedly, connections have been made between the design of justice 'systems' and design theory more generally. The next chapter broadens the discussion to encompass that wider culture and to reflect in particular on urban planning and the design of public space. It aims to find in that broader culture not just recognisably similar trajectories of optimism and disappointment, but options for a more democratic reimagining of public value that are transferable to the particular practices of human rights and administrative justice.

References

Adler, M. (Ed.). (2010). *Administrative Justice in Context*. Oxford: Hart.

Adler, M. (2012). The Rise and Fall of Administrative Justice—A Cautionary Tale. *Socio-Legal Review, 8*, 29–54.

Adler, M. (2018). *Cruel, Inhuman or Degrading Treatment: Benefit Sanctions in the UK*. London: Palgrave Pivot.

Administrative Justice and Tribunals Council (AJTC). (2010). *Principles of Administrative Justice*. London: AJTC.

Bondy, V., & Doyle, M. (2011). *Mediation in Judicial Review: A Practical Handbook for Lawyers*. London: Public Law Project.

Bondy, V., & Le Sueur, A. (2012). *Designing Redress: A Study about Grievances against Public Bodies*. London: Public Law Project.

Bondy, V., & Sunkin, M. (2009). *The Dynamics of Judicial Review Litigation: The Resolution of Public Law Challenges before Final Hearing*. London: Public Law Project.

Bondy, V., et al. (2009). *Mediation and Judicial Review: An Empirical Research Study*. London: Public Law Project.

Bondy, V., Platt, L., & Sunkin, M. (2015). *The Value and Effects of Judicial Review: The Nature of Claims, Their Outcomes and Consequences*. London: Public Law Project.

Bottomore, T. (1992). Citizenship and Social Class, Forty Years On. In T. H. Marshall & T. Bottomore (Eds.), *Citizenship and Social Class*. London: Pluto.

Creutzfeldt, N. (2018). *Ombudsmen and ADR: A Comparative Study of Informal Justice in Europe*. Geneva: Palgrave Macmillan.

Drewry, G. (2009). The Judicialisation of 'Administrative' Tribunals in the UK: From Hewart to Legatt. *Transylvanian Review of Administrative Sciences, 28*, 45–64.

Equality and Human Rights Commission (EHRC). (2008). *The Role and Experience of Inspectorates, Regulators and Complaints-Handling Bodies in Promoting Human Rights Standards in Public Services*. London: Equality and Human Rights Commission.

Equality and Human Rights Commission (EHRC). (2014). *Human Rights in Action: Case Studies for Regulators, Inspectorates and Ombudsmen*. London: Equality and Human Rights Commission.

Fredman, S. (2011). *Discrimination Law* (2nd ed.). Oxford: OUP.

Gearty, C. (2016). *On Fantasy Island: Britain, Europe and Human Rights*. Oxford: OUP.

Gearty, C., & Mantouvlou, V. (2011). *Debating Social Rights*. Oxford: Hart.

Gill, C., Mullen, T., & Vivian, N. (2019). *The Managerial Ombuds* (forthcoming).

Halliday, S., & Schmidt, P. (Eds.). (2004). *Human Rights Brought Home: Socio-Legal Perspectives on Human Rights in the National Context*. Oxford: Hart.

Hammarberg, T. (2007a). *Speech to the EU Ombudsmen Network*. Athens, Greece.

Hammarberg, T. (2007b). *Les Droits de l'Homme en Europe: Mission Inaccomplie*. Strasbourg: Council of Europe.

Herring, J. (2017). Compassion, Ethics of Care and Legal Rights. *International Journal of Law in Context, 13*(2), 158–171.

Hertogh, M. (2018). *Nobody's Law: Legal Consciousness and Legal Alienation in Everyday Life*. Geneva: Palgrave Macmillan.

Hewart, L. C. J. (1929). *The New Despotism*. London: Ernest Benn.

Horwitz, M. (1977). The Rule of Law: An Unqualified Human Good? *Yale Law Journal, 86*, 561–566.

Hunt, P. (2017). *Social Rights are Human Rights—But the UK System is Rigged*. London: Centre for Welfare Reform.
King, J. (2012). *Judging Social Rights*. Cambridge: CUP.
Klug, F. (2000). *Values for a Godless Age: The Story of the United Kingdom's New Bill of Rights*. Harmondsworth: Penguin.
Labour Party. (1964). *The New Britain*. London: Labour Party.
Marshall, T. H. (1992). Citizenship and Social Class. In T. H. Marshall & T. Bottomore (Eds.), *Citizenship and Social Class*. London: Pluto.
Moyn, S. (2018). *Not Enough: Human Rights in an Unequal World*. Cambridge, MA: Harvard University Press.
Mulcahy, L. (2013). The Collective Interest in Private Dispute Resolution. *Oxford Journal of Legal Studies, 33*, 59–80.
Nonet, P., & Selznick, P. (1978). *Toward Responsive Law: Law and Society in Transition*. New York: Harper Torch.
O'Hara, G. (2012). *Governing Post-war Britain: The Paradoxes of Progress*. Geneva: Palgrave Macmillan.
Richards, Z. (2019). *Responsive Legality: The New Administrative Justice*. Abingdon and New York: Routledge.
Sossin, L. (2017). Designing Administrative Justice. *Windsor Yearbook of Access to Justice, 34*(1), 87–111.
Stacey, F. (1971). *The British Ombudsman*. Oxford: Clarendon Press.
Street, H. (1975). *Justice in the Welfare State* (Hamlyn Lecture, 20th series) (2nd ed.). London: Stevens.
Sugarman, D. (1986). Legal Theory, the Common Law Mind and the Making of the Textbook Tradition. In W. Twining (Ed.), *Legal Theory and Common Law*. Oxford: Blackwell.
Titmuss, R. (1971). Welfare 'Rights', Law and Discretion. *Political Quarterly, 42*, 113–132.
Tomkins, A. (2005). *Our Republican Constitution*. Oxford: Hart.
Tomlinson, J. (2017). The Grammar of Administrative Justice Values. *Journal of Social Welfare and Family Law, 39*(4), 524–537.
White Paper: *Transforming Public Services: Complaints, Redress and Tribunals*. (2004). London: Department for Constitutional Affairs.
Zacka, B. (2017). *When the State Meets the Street: Public Service and Moral Agency*. Cambridge, MA: Harvard University Press.

CHAPTER 4

Designing for Democratic Engagement

Abstract This chapter shifts the focus to the broader post-war design culture. It considers the way in which urban design and planning met challenges similar to those encountered by administrative justice and human rights during the same period and explains how alternatives to the priorities of individual user, system and closure were expressed in the values of community, network and openness. The post-war vogue for Scandi-design, the celebrations of the Festival of Britain and the contested territory between the 'new humanists' and the 'new brutalists' emerge as directly relevant to contemporary options for administrative justice in an age characterised by a 'digital by default' mentality.

Keywords Community • Network • Openness • Design history • Consumerism • Participation

New Ideal Design Principles

The grip in which legalism and neoliberalism have held social rights and administrative justice has resulted in the prioritisation of principles of individual user, system and closure, principles that limit the scope for democratic engagement and hollow out the common good. This chapter considers how insights from design history and current developments in design thinking illuminate the options for reimagining administrative justice

M. Doyle, N. O'Brien, *Reimagining Administrative Justice*,
https://doi.org/10.1007/978-3-030-21388-6_4

in partnership with social rights and for developing new ideal design principles. In doing so, it explores the wider design culture in twentieth-century Britain, and in particular the role of the state in sponsoring and implementing design standards, the shifting relationship of designer and user, and the introduction of new design methods that seek to address a democratic deficit and to reposition the role of users—as a collective rather than as individuals, and as co-creators rather than passive recipients.

The discussion draws on key moments in design history. The state's role in design was a significant and benevolent force in the period after World War II both as a commissioner of design initiatives and as a source of standard setting and regulation. Of particular symbolic importance is the Festival of Britain of 1951 and its embrace of Scandi-design as an expression of the social democratic moment that also saw the introduction of the ombud institution into British life. Over the subsequent decades, changes in consumer power and the dynamic between user and designer altered the understanding of 'user focus', but design developments also brought new ideas about the public realm that are useful to draw on in reimagining administrative justice. Critiques of court and civic architecture and more recent moves towards virtual justice provide insights into changing perceptions of the citizen-state relationship and the realisation of ideals of transparency and accountability. More widely, lessons can be drawn from the emergence of urban planning—the interface with democracy at local level (Minton 2012)—as a discipline generating fresh ideas from architects committed to public housing, schools and town halls and as an area which, like administrative justice, is made up of everyday 'small places' and encounters between citizen and state and which also urgently needs reassertion of democratic and humane values.

What is Design, and Why Does It Matter?

'Design' is often associated with style and with objects, with fashion and products. Yet design reaches much further into our lives if we consider it as a 'mode' of thinking, one that allows us to imagine how things could be, not just how they are. Design thinker Ezio Manzini describes this mode as requiring three senses: the critical (being able to identify what is not acceptable, what needs changing); the creative (being able to imagine what does not exist, or at least not yet); and the practical (being able to identify feasible ways to make change happen). He links it to the concept of capability, as a mode of thinking that 'points to a positive way toward human progress, meaning the possibility of developing our most specifically human talents… compatible with a scenario in which people reflect on what they wish to do and be' (Manzini 2015: 32). Democracy itself is both a product of design (the 'what') and an exercise in design (the 'how'); good design facilitates democratic participation and is a 'catalyst for driving positive cultural and social change' (Narkiewicz-Laine undated). It should take us further than the anodyne promise of 'human-centred design' toward something more akin to 'humanist design' and its potential 'to promote an authentic democracy in the contemporary world' (Bonsiepe 2010: 63).

In this wider sense, design applies to systems, procedures, institutions and relationships as much as to objects. It is about problem-solving, but not only that—increasingly it is about the social necessity of making sense, and of doing so in a collective, participatory and democratic way. Design in this sense is 'a culture and a practice concerning how things ought to be in order to attain desired functions and meanings' (Manzini 2015: 53). It occurs within an open-ended process involving a range of design 'actors'. Echoing the capabilities approach developed by Amartya Sen and Martha Nussbaum, the expectation is that everyone can, with support from others if necessary, draw on their own 'capability' to participate fully. Such an expectation reflects a shift from a twentieth-century focus primarily on industrial and technological production and towards, instead, the need to recognise 'design' as a collective and collaborative activity, the need to involve a wider network of 'design participants', and the need to be open-ended rather than closed.

Systematising the Ad Hoc

Two examples illustrate the importance of design for function and meaning, and in particular of the state's role as design commissioner and of the emergence of 'system design' as the preferred response to ad hoc development. Design approaches of the mid-twentieth century, in administrative justice as in housing and the built environment, were not characterised by collaboration or participation but by the imposition of design principles by identified experts. The Franks Committee's review of administrative tribunals, published in 1957, was one of the first attempts by the state at justice system design. It radically changed the perception and status of tribunals, moving them from within government administration closer to the independent judiciary and identifying core common law principles of openness, fairness and impartiality. It was, in many ways, the first attempt to impose a 'system' onto the varied institutions that had developed in an incremental way over the previous decades. As already suggested, the legacy of Franks was in effect the creeping judicialisation of the tribunal system which would gather pace after the 2004 White Paper and the Tribunals, Courts and Enforcement Act 2007.

In a parallel design initiative, the same year as the Franks Report, the UK government oversaw a radical overhaul of road signage in Britain. The Preston Bypass (which became Britain's first motorway) was due to open in 1958 as part of an ambitious road-building initiative. Increasingly concerned about road safety amid a dramatic increase in car ownership and the confusing array of signs directing motorists, the government set up the Anderson Committee to look into models for a signage 'system' to be rolled out across all Britain's roads, a task overseen by the subsequent Worboys Committee. This was one of the most ambitious projects for information design in Britain at the time, and the system designed by graphic designers Jock Kinneir and Margaret Calvert is not only still in use today on Britain's roads but has influenced the design decisions taken by the Government Digital Service in creating the gov.uk platform used for all UK government websites (Terrett 2012a).

The modernising and systematic ambitions apparent in both Franks and Worboys are a revealing illustration of the way in which in the 1950s a common cultural context informed the reform of both administrative justice and the shaping of public space. Yet despite those similar ambitions, it is apparent that the material upon which state-sponsored design initiatives were put to work was very different in each case, with very different results. In the case of highway signage, uniformity and 'system' were achieved by giving expression to contemporary Modernist ideals of purity and clarity, unshackled by the accumulated messiness of incremental development and history. For administrative justice, the move towards judicialisation was an acknowledgement that 'system' went hand in hand with increasing legalism and the appearance of coherence that the accumulated common law offered.

Design for the 'Good Life'

The conservative revolution of the Garden City movement provides necessary background to the post-war housing initiatives of the emerging welfare state. Its own roots are in the late nineteenth-century creation of utopian model villages by factory owners and philanthropists concerned about the conditions of their workers. These included Saltaire, built by mill owner Titus Salt outside Bradford in the 1850s, and Port Sunlight, near Liverpool, built in 1888 by soap factory owner William Hesketh Lever, who wanted his workers' village to reflect the qualities of the soap they helped produce and that was marketed as fresh, healthy and satisfying—the good life as clean and pure, as carefully crafted as an advertisement for Sunlight Soap and drawing on the same 'optimistic, cosmetic priorities' (Yallop 2015: 168).

Ebenezer Howard's Garden City idea, while sharing some of the ideals of the 'good life' with Saltaire and Port Sunlight, was more forward-looking in his vision of a new society that addressed the problems faced by both urban congestion and rural exodus. The city was overgrown and overcrowded, with many living in dire conditions, while the country had 'fresh air, sunlight, pleasant vistas' but also 'a sort of destitution, a dearth of human companionship and of co-operative effort' (Mumford, in Howard 1965: 33). Howard referred to the Garden City as a third alternative, a way to secure the benefits of both town and country, urban energy and activity along with rural beauty and delight, 'in perfect combination' (Howard 1965: 45–46). His diagram of the 'three magnets'—town, country, and town-country—shows the advantages and disadvantages of the rivalling city and country magnets, with the town-country magnet as free from all disadvantages and also, with land owned co-operatively, as a break from 'old economic structures and social hierarchies' (Yallop 2015: 178).

Howard's emphasis on liveability and on principles of self-governance and self-administration made him a revolutionary, somewhat 'like a cross between Karl Marx and William Morris' (Hanley 2017: 57), a radical whose vision was steeped in concerns for social justice but also deeply conservative and paternalistic. Letchworth Garden City, for example, has been said to have inaugurated a housing model that separated spaces into serving and served in the home 'as the appropriate moral framework for the nation' (Mae Architects 2014: 12). The Garden City's sustainability relied on an imposed discipline, harmony through order, stripping citizens of agency to shape their environs (Sennett 2018: 85). Urban thinker Jane Jacobs has written scathingly of Howard's vision as aiming to create 'really very nice small towns if you were docile and had no plans of your own and did not mind spending your life among others with no plans of their own. As in all Utopias, the right to have plans of any significance belonged only to the planners in charge' (Jacobs 2000: 27). Yet the impact of Howard's ideas can be seen in the great home-building efforts between the wars

(Hanley 2017: 51): much of this 'design for the good life' lay the ground for the vision of the architects of Britain's welfare state, in which it was 'assumed that benevolent experts would organise services for citizens…in their best interests' and that citizens accepted the underlying premises of shared public interest on which the welfare state was founded (Griffiths and Kippin 2013: 2).

The Public Sector as Design Standard Setter

Government-led design dominated design initiatives in the first half of the twentieth century, fuelled by the emerging disciplines of urban planning and industrial design. Design had a political force and became a means of expressing the new relationship between state and citizen, from clearing slum housing and building new homes and schools for a growing population to improving the design of home furnishings in times of austerity. The decades following World War II were particularly important for designers in Britain, with the government supporting initiatives to bring design to the people and establish design standards while at the same time boosting the country's profile as an exporter of design. The Victoria & Albert Museum hosted the *Britain Can Make It* exhibition in 1946, aimed at generating interest in design standards among the general public but primarily focused on international buyers. Transport authorities (airports, railways, the London Underground, the Ministry of Public Buildings and Works) were among the first to pick up on the importance of design for the public sector and the need to develop design policies (McCarthy 1982). The Council of Industrial Design was formed in 1944 and the Arts Council of Great Britain in 1946; funded from central government, both bodies 'exemplified the belief in government intervention, control and planning' (Jackson 2002).

The Utility Scheme, established by the Board of Trade in 1942 to regulate the design, manufacture and sale of furniture during World War II, when many essential commodities were rationed, was 'a quite unprecedented example of state intervention in regulating standards of design' (McCarthy 1982: 123). It also offered 'a social opportunity of the first order', relying on the force that only a government monopoly could muster to bring about change in public taste toward a Modernist minimalism (Woodham 1997: 118). Although the Scheme lingered on long after the War, until 1952, its cause of taking good design to the masses was hampered by the fact that the masses appeared to reject its 'less is more' adage (Woodham 1997: 118).

Despite the unpopularity of the Utility Scheme, in the period immediately following the War the setting of standards of good design, in housing and urban planning, in textiles and everyday homewares, became a shared preoccupation and led to collaborations between government and designers that were unprecedented. Design had a moral and ethical dimension that linked it with the changing society and political reforms of Attlee's post-war Labour government. This shared interest in standard setting (reflected too in the developing of principles for administrative justice initiated with the 1957 Franks Report) found colourful new expression with Scandinavian design and the 'pleasant time', as design historian Fiona McCarthy describes it, 'when standards seemed so certain, and good design meant comeliness and usefulness and sense' (McCarthy 1972: 178). Users, ordinary people, began to take an interest in design standards: 'The British began paying more attention to detail: to good lettering on captions and on signposts, to interior and exterior furniture, electrical fitments, litter-bins and landscaping, to texture and the colour of paving and to lighting, things which they had hardly bothered with before' (McCarthy 1972: 175).

Scandi-Design and the Festival of Britain

The growing interest in Britain of Scandinavian design marked the beginning of a new role for the end user and was linked with a desire to humanise the expanding state bureaucracy after the War (as exemplified in the introduction from Scandinavia of the ombud institution in the late 1960s). Scandinavian design, and chiefly Danish design, of the mid-twentieth century was seen as accessible, warm, and able 'to humanise what had been standardised' (Mussari 2016: 3). An interest in 'users' and their comfort, and the interaction of 'user' and object, set Scandinavian designers apart from those focused primarily on function.

The influence of Scandinavia in the 1950s and 1960s went well beyond the political idealisation of the Nordic welfare states after the war, especially in the thinking of Labour intellectuals such as Crosland and Crossman and in the development of Labour's policy on wages, education and administrative justice, especially with the introduction of the ombud (O'Hara 2008a). Suddenly the adornment so craved in the austere Utility Scheme years was out, and the public's imagination was captured instead by the clean lines and democratic foundations of Scandinavian domestic design: 'everywhere you went, you were almost sure of finding a Svensk or Norsk or Dansk shop, full of stainless steel and teak' (McCarthy 1972: 183).

The Festival of Britain expressed much of this Scandinavian allure, not least in its democratic ideals and its intention to look forward while not abandoning past traditions still held in deep affection. It was intended to mark the centenary of the Great Exhibition of 1851 and that event's success in promoting British exports. Gerald Barry, a journalist who was appointed Director-General of the Festival, described it as 'British democracy in action', both in its contents ('design for the people') and in the way it was conceived as a joint effort of government-appointed committees, existing voluntary organisations, and local communities to improve design standards. Rooted in the social democratic ideals of the post-war Attlee government, the Festival had an overtly socialist message: design as a humanising force, 'real things for real people' (McCarthy 2014: 117), reflecting urban planning and design principles but with a hint of whimsy, incorporating architecture, sculpture, typography and product design, all 'for the people'. They were interwoven contributions; the built environment, housing and transport relied on textiles in particular to humanise them; design of household objects made real the promise that good design was within reach of all.

This hankering for humanising features after the horrors of the War is symbolised by the prevalence of wood as a finish for the interiors of the Royal Festival Hall, which was, in the words of Finnish designer Arno Aalto, 'better for the human touch'. Town planning and architecture were prominent, 'to attempt something more dynamic, which would lend these somewhat specialist subjects an appeal to the understanding and imagination of the ordinary citizen, whose life, although he (sic) seldom realises it, they so intimately affect' (Barry 1952: 684). An example is the Lansbury Estate, built in London's East End community of Poplar, which had been badly damaged in the War. The Estate became the Festival's Live Architecture Exhibition, with a design based on a Continental European feel of blocks of flats, terraced houses, open spaces, and a central market square. Susan Lawrence School, a new primary school for the Lansbury community, was designed to be at human scale, with light and openness and colourful features including Peggy Angus's Festival-yellow tile designs. Carolyn Trant, Angus's biographer, writes of the passionate commitment of Angus and her fellow artists at the time 'to make a better world and society' (quoted in Russell 2014: 7).

New Humanists and New Brutalists

Rebuilding after the War focused on structures that were fundamental to the state making a better life for its citizens—on schools, public housing, civic centres. Different schools of architectural thought battled for primacy in such urgent, large-scale and high-profile projects. As historian Glen O'Hara has observed, as a result of the influence exercised by Scandinavia over the British mid-century mind, debates in contemporary architecture were 'played out around different views of Swedish design', with more determined Modernists largely despising the 'faltering humanism' of the Festival and the 'small-scale compromises' of Scandinavian style (O'Hara 2008b: 9).

Modernism had a profound ethical base founded on its designers' belief that surroundings and the built environment affect how people live and relate to each other. In *Toward a New Architecture*, Le Corbusier wrote that architecture is a medium that most literally allows for influence on daily life and political engagement. He and other Modernists were community-minded; they aimed for ideal forms (in buildings and artworks) that went beyond (even ignored) the individual herself and individual preferences. But Modernism in its pure form failed to take hold in Britain, its use of concrete and steel in its 'streets in the sky' leading to alienation and its prescriptive adherence to rules restricting personal freedoms in the face of mass media and new technologies (Woodham 1997). The counterpoint to the omniscient viewpoint adopted by Modernist architects was the street-level perspective for which urban thinker Jane Jacobs campaigned. Hers is an organic city shaped by its inhabitants, not the other way around. Whereas for Le Corbusier houses were 'machines for living', for Jacobs they were adaptable nests responding to the way people live: 'Form will emerge from the way people dwell', celebrated sociologist Richard Sennett writes of Jacob's views, in which 'function' 'stands for the host of informal, free, loose, activities occurring face to face' (Sennett 2018: 81). Her 'dance of the streets', the unchoreographed encounters of neighbours and strangers, is implicitly recognised in Manzini's design for social innovation, a design mode that embraces neighbourhood management, care activities and community building as activities that 'constitute the basic fabric of day-to-day quality of life' (Manzini 2015: 24) and which has as its building blocks complexity, openness, connectivity, collaboration and capabilities.

The 'Scandi versus Modernist' architectural debate was personified in Britain in a 'fierce rivalry' between two couples who embraced distinct schools of architectural thought: Scandi-influenced Mary and David Medd and 'New Brutalists' Alison and Peter Smithson (Grindrod 2013: 129). The Medds worked with Hertfordshire local authority to build pre-fab schools to meet the needs of the growing population (which included four New Towns); they worked with education officers to observe pupil behaviour, incorporated colourful tiles and textiles, and introduced new layouts, placing teachers at the centre rather than front of the classroom. The Smithsons built the first 'New Brutalist' school, Hunstanton Secondary Modern, a stark black Modernist structure of glass and exposed steel. It was a 'direct reaction against…the dominant Scandinavian style of the day', a style characterised as the 'effete toff' in contrast with New Brutalism's 'plain-speaking and authentic' hero (Grindrod 2013: 140–141).

In this contest, the 'New Humanists' largely prevailed, at least in the short term. Even the Conservative Government of 1959–64 adopted, with mixed results, housing policies from Scandinavia, notably co-operatives subsidized by the state but managed by owners and tenants. In the event, the sort of successful coalition of builders, buyers and tenants achieved in Scandinavia eluded successful 'transfer' to Britain, and by the 1970s the Scandinavian 'economic miracle' had lost much of its allure for British policy makers. Nevertheless, this break with native approaches was indicative of the extent to which Scandinavia had become in public policy circles a touchstone for an oxymoronic form of 'conservative' innovation, one that resonates in administrative justice reform today.

The New User and the Decline of the Public Realm

This change in domestic taste after the War can be seen as a turning point, one rooted in the need not just to solve problems (problems of post-war shortage, for example) but to achieve 'meaning'. This pursuit of meaning, or 'sense-making', as it is described by design theorist Ezio Manzini, inevitably entailed a different role for the ordinary citizen, or end-user, and a new approach that offered the prospect of more democratic participation in the interests of the common good whilst also creating the possibility of a more individualistic ethos and louder 'consumer voice'.

As the economy improved and people's disposable income increased, by the late 1950s the consumerist approach began to hold sway, with designers increasingly abandoning their principled approach and catering to the demands of the buyer: 'Design became an agent of consumerism and, in an economy based upon free enterprise, the possibility of design remaining a servant of moral or ethical standpoints seemed increasingly remote' (Jackson 2002). As McCarthy notes of the shift in the late 1950s, 'Design was advertising; Design was serious commerce' (McCarthy 1972: 181–182). The effect on designers was to force them to take account increasingly of behavioural science and ergonomics; they could no longer rely on 'designer knows best' but had to collaborate with industry and with users in new ways, to be one of many agents. 'Systematic methods' of design, the focus of a conference in London in 1962 that was 'a milestone in British design history' (McCarthy 1982: 145), aimed to break down barriers between artist and designer, designer and engineer, engineer and user. 'Design' as a term began to be applied to more than products and buildings, including services and working environments, and design was increasingly professionalised. The role was still important in contributing to social change, but the designer was no longer social reformer but 'interpreter of social aspirations' (McCarthy 1982: 149).

The shift from design 'user' to design 'consumer', the 'alluring image of consumerism' and the freedom to express one's individual taste through lifestyle design (Woodham 1997: 121) coincided with a decline in the public realm, including housing and urban spaces, through privatisation and market forces, and a resulting decline in democratic accountability (Minton 2012). The public interest that underpinned planning and the welfare state was at its peak in the decades following World War II, but 'its rise was swiftly followed by its fall', the idealism of the post-war building programme in the end defeated by the 'undemocratic nature' of the initiatives, however well intentioned (Minton 2012). Use of poor-quality materials was part of this undemocratic nature, the collapse of housing block Ronan Point in 1968 a tragic example. Another issue was that post-war planning segregated low- and higher-income households; it prioritised 'originality over other values such as memory, familiarity or a responsibility to its wider setting' (Mae Architects 2014: 32). It was missing the 'glue' that holds communities together, a glue that was further eroded by the Right to Buy policy of the early 1980s, a policy that coincided with the scrapping of mandatory space standards for public housing that were developed in the 1960s by the government's Parker Morris Committee in an attempt to keep pace with rising living standards.

Council housing built between the wars was not marked out as 'social housing' in terms of appearance or cosmetics; the ambition of the planners and architects was to provide well-designed homes for all people, and it was not until later that Council housing acquired the stigma that still attaches to it today (Hanley 2017: 65). By then, housing for the poor or working classes began to be 'set apart from speculative builders who deal with the better-off', something denounced by Minister for Health and Housing Aneurin Bevan as early as 1946, when he spoke of 'colonies' and of 'a monstrous infliction upon the essential psychological and biological one-ness of the community' (Mae Architects 2014: 32–33). The failure to realise the post-war ambitions of a good life for all were therefore only partly due to the machine-like vision of the Modernists and New Brutalists. Although the modern UK planning system emerged at the same time as the welfare state, it was vulnerable to capture by the forces unleashed by the consumer ethos and privatisation brought in with neoliberalism in the 1970s.

A stark example of this capture of planning, and of the limitations of closure, is the creation of what journalist and academic Anna Minton refers to as 'pseudo-public' and 'pseudo-private' realms, predominantly but not solely in our urban environments. Minton, who calls for 'a new constitutional settlement that will put the idea of the public good back at the centre of the public realm' (Minton 2012: xxxvii), describes 'pseudo-public' space as privately owned but open to the public (such as a shopping mall owned by private-sector landlords), and 'pseudo-private' space as public land managed by private contractors (such as Business Improvement Districts outsourced by local authorities). The Faustian deal made by local authorities in such arrangements is that streets are kept clean and safe (although these are contentious values, as Minton notes, reflecting questions of who the 'user' is—safe for whom?) in exchange for private, and publicly unaccountable, control over who can use them and how. One consequence is that loitering or lingering, what might be referred to as 'doing nothing', is designed out (Minton 2012: 53).

Considering these changes to the way public spaces are controlled, Minton rebuts arguments that the privatisation of public spaces (turning urban streets into malls controlled by Business Improvement Districts, for example) is what people want, that citizens are predominantly consumers. She argues that this approach, this way of creating places, has not been part of the political debate, so most people remain unaware of the role of private companies in managing the public realm. In other ways, too, the 'pseudo-private space' that Minton describes challenges the democracy of the public realm in constraining open disagreement. Aristotle, Sennett writes, argued that a democratic space is an open one: 'the ideal size of a city should be one in which a shout at one end could be heard at the other', and cities are 'most alive when debate is open and fractious and things happen' (Sennett 2018: 82).

Where Justice Happens

The second half of the twentieth century is predominantly a period of privatisation of space and decline of the public. It was also a period of redefining the citizen-state relationship; like the new consumer, the 'new citizen' was expected to assert voice and preference, the new administration was a service provider. Civic and court architecture reflected this shift. Victorian Town Halls, with their imposing entrances, 'represent the era's paternalistic relationship between power and public: patronizing, but also somehow comforting'. The post-war Council office or Town Hall lacks grand entrances and public gathering spaces and has 'a very different understanding of its duties, changing the focus from charity to obligation, particularly in perception' (McCormick 2014). Council offices built from the 1960s on were 'not meant to join the public and the administration through visibility, but to process mass public need'. The architectural style of concrete Brutalism, even the more humanistic New Brutalism, often got the blame for people's unfriendly reception, but the style of building reflected the changed administrative intent. In other words, 'The architecture did not create the myth of the "faceless bureaucrat" but it certainly gave it a distinctive aesthetic' (McCormick 2014).

As far as where 'justice' happens, it may be fair to say that administrative justice, popularly perceived to be rooted in bureaucratic decision-making, tends to happen in office buildings and complexes, 'rarely marked at street level, rarely located where most of their users live and work', with a look and feel that 'might be characterised charitably as "bureaucratic"' (Sossin 2017: 15). Grander premises for justice, such as courts and parliament buildings, hold out loftier ambitions in their duty to the public and public spaces; they are not just 'machines for the administration of justice' but they should instead express 'our shared values'. As features of a democratic society, buildings should themselves be 'democratic' spaces where all citizens can feel 'free to roam, learn and participate' (Rogers 2017: 207). Debates about good design have been expressed in the design of the court estate both in the UK and elsewhere, involving issues of openness and privacy, authority and participation, modernity and tradition, mechanism and humanism. In the post-war period, and especially since the 1960s, the old

Victorian courthouses designed to express the 'majesty of the law', and epitomised in the high-gothic Royal Courts of Justice on the Strand in London, have been subjected to what has been described as a 'democratic turn' (Mulcahy 2011: 142). As part of that democratic turn, court buildings have had an important role in mediating and reflecting this new 'political compact', with democracy and equality the dominant ideals.

Although architects of the post-war period may have succeeded in expressing a Modernist vision and so breaking with tradition, as with many of the designers of large social housing projects, the attempt to create buildings that were 'accessible and inviting' was less successful (Mulcahy 2011: 144). As a result, later Court Service guidance emphasised the quality of 'openness' and the need to 'temper the designer's approach' with recognition of the needs of occasional users of the buildings, whose attendance at court was likely to be 'rare and perhaps disturbing' (Mulcahy 2011: 145). A new philosophy gradually emerged that emphasised equality over authority: 'The scales of justice are a more appropriate symbol than the sword of retribution' (Mulcahy 2011: 145). Yet even the new 'open' dispensation has failed to meet all expectations. The Manchester Civil Justice Centre, for example, has been regarded as the 'flagship' of the new court estate in Britain since its completion in 2008. Yet even its tenor of 'civic generosity' has not escaped the more general critique of contemporary design that it fails to reflect principles of accessibility and fairness and lacks 'civic presence'. Its spaces are open and airy, but like Le Corbusier's Chandigarh court complex, it has a clinical feel, underscored by its lack of artwork or any human touch. This is true also of architect Richard Rogers' Antwerp Law Courts, whose internal walkways are made of glass so judges and the public can see each other as they walk on adjoining walkways, producing a 'powerful symbol of accountability' (Mulcahy 2011: 153). Despite the prevalence of wood and glass in the ship-like design, and the presence of several hulking bronze sculptures, the law courts feel uninviting and unpeopled. Nevertheless, these law courts, Manchester and Antwerp, 'challenge fossilized design templates and find new ways for courthouses to acquire integrity as public spaces' (Mulcahy 2011: 153).

Architects grapple with the balance to be achieved between individual user-choice and the broader public good, and in that way they confront issues similar to those faced by designers of administrative justice. Rogers, for example, invites reconsideration of who the 'user' is and includes within its compass the casual 'user' who might not even regard herself as a 'user' at all: 'For architecture to enhance the city and civic life, it needs to consider more than the client's immediate requirements. The architect must consider the building's users, and the passers-by, asking like Louis Khan, What could this building be? What should it be? What will it add to the city?' (Rogers 2017: 207). Rogers' vision as a practitioner is to that extent aligned with much of the contemporary theoretician's striving for the 'open city', for 'porous boundaries', for Aristotelian diversity within shared public space, for inter-connection and participation, an element of 'friction' and, critically, 'not too much user-friendliness' (Sennett 2018).

A vision of the 'humanised' legal setting from a legal practitioner's rather than an architect's perspective is captured in the words of Albie Sachs, former President of the South African Constitutional Court. Describing the post-apartheid Constitutional Court building in Johannesburg, with its sculpture and tapestries, 'integrated artworks' that included carpets, chandeliers and embroideries, and the use of natural light and air, he wrote: 'The law can be very cold, arid, clinical, artificial and remote, or it can be very human-centred—concerned with discovering points of good in society, ways of moving forward, of respecting the autonomy of the individual and social solidarity and human interconnection at the same time' (Sachs 2007: 96). The impact of an environment that expresses those competing qualities is to 'humanise' the work that the Court does, as 'part and parcel of a vision and an approach to life' that aims at 'an intense sense of humanity and a strong preoccupation with human dignity' (Sachs 2007: 96). This is a court quite simply designed for social justice.

Design Thinking and Digital Justice

In the twenty-first century, as the places where administrative justice happens are changing and becoming virtual, new challenges arise in relation to openness (is a virtual hearing room an 'open' one?) and to accountability (how does one challenge a decision made by artificial intelligence?). Master of the Rolls Lord Etherington has made it clear that hearing rooms are a thing of the past: 'we can reconfigure the design of our court buildings because traditional court rooms will only be required where such an environment is necessary for resolution of the dispute in a world where digital adjudication is otherwise available' (Etherington 2017). The UK Government's ambition, announced in 2010, to be 'digital by default', to have all government services managed and accessed online, presented similar challenges to that faced by the Anderson and Worboys committees and designers Kinnear and Calvert in achieving a total redesign of the motorway signage system—addressing the problems of a confusing and chaotic landscape by imposing a unified, consistent system with clear information as its primary goal—'swap signage systems for websites. Swap vehicle traffic for online traffic' (Terrett 2012b).

The Government Digital Service (GDS), a cross-government team based in the Cabinet Office, is now a key player in design of administrative justice (Tomlinson 2017); it is also an example of 'agile' design in action, an element of what is called 'design thinking', an approach to design that is iterative, with a focus on usability and user focus achieved through employing empathy, observation, discovery, and defining, testing, evaluating and evolving (Sossin 2017; Tomlinson 2017). Design thinking emerged in the 1960s and 1970s, but it is only recently that it has gained traction within design of justice systems; now it 'is increasingly important within the administrative justice sector, and forms part of the new political and policy dynamics emerging within the digitalisation agenda' (Tomlinson 2017). Taking a lead on the justice reform programme set out in the government's Transforming Our Justice System White Paper (2016), GDS took the position that it needed to focus on user needs and work in an agile, iterative and human-focused way, to recognise the centrality of people, which means that unlike in many other software development projects there is little upfront planning. In administrative justice, design thinking asks different questions than those posed by traditional discussions of justice design; it takes a holistic approach and links these legal design issues with those of user need and of resources (Sossin 2017).

There are reasons to be cautious in light of design thinking optimism, however, not least the question of how far it can be implemented in the administrative justice context of constrained 'system costs' and, more onerously, whether it represents 'the further encroachment of neoliberalism and the logic of the market on the public sector' (Tomlinson 2017). One response to these concerns may be to remind ourselves of the purpose of design, or rather its purposes. Design thinking is often talked of as an approach to address 'wicked' problems, a term used by Richard Buchanan in the early 1990s to describe problems that are complex, poorly defined and challenging. But design is not only about solving problems; it is also about sense-making, which inevitably involves questions of culture, of language and meaning, and of relationships (Manzini 2015). Problem-solving and sense-making necessarily co-exist, influencing each other: one asks will it work (will the problem be solved?) and the second asks what it will mean to the user. In this conception, every artefact (technological device, invention, service) tells two stories. The reason design thinking is so appropriate for administrative justice is its importance in telling many stories, not only those of how to address citizen grievance but also those of how to advance policy, and often highly political, aims.

Designing for Administrative Justice: 'Community', 'Networks' and 'Openness'

The preceding discussion gives a flavour of post-war debates as they have affected design standards and the public realm and illuminated tensions between individual choice and the common good and between social democratic citizenship and the market. Administrative justice, despite its extra-judicial aspirations, had during the same period been shaped by design ideals of legalism and consumerism that prioritised the individual user, the desirability of system and the aspiration for closure. Taking a cue from Manzini's work on design for social innovation, we propose that design culture can provide an alternative framework of community, network and openness.

First, there is the centrality of community as a counterweight to individual choice. The immediate post-war idealisation of the state and desire to serve the common good came under increasing pressure from the interests of the individual user conceived as a 'consumer', especially in the context of expanding markets and dispersed affluence. Part of the appeal of Scandinavian society and politics was its apparent harnessing of the best of both worlds, due regard to the individual being preserved without jettisoning the broader ideals of the good society. Moreover, Scandinavian design appeared to marry the old with the new in a way that more severe models of Modernism did not. The appeal of such a compromise to a peculiarly Romantic form of Modernism in Britain is readily apparent (Harris 2010). Apparent too is the abiding tension between individual and the common good in attempts to find new ways of enabling democratic participation.

Yet in all the design innovations discussed, whether Garden Cities, the Festival of Britain, post-war social housing policy and court design, there is an abiding realisation that community interests must be recognised if the aspiration of 'design for living' is to fulfil its potential. The humanising ambition of design entails respect for the 'relational self' rather than acquiescence in the worship of the 'atomised individual'.

Secondly, there is the importance of networks as an alternative to system. If 'system' implies hard borders, severe boundaries, control, order and consistency, the notion of network implies something softer, more fluid and potentially more complex and unpredictable. The idea of the networked environment evokes aspirations towards co-ordination rather than prescription, and the need for connection, not separation, integration rather than segregation. Regulatory networks not only seek to replace command-and-control approaches, but to adapt the insights of reflexive regulation for a more nuanced and agile social environment. To that extent, networked governance is more than just the 'new governance' of the last quarter of the twentieth century. It is an attempt to remodel relationships of power so that they take account of the complexity of contemporary institutional structures, methods and modes of communication.

Porous boundaries, shared space, and resistance to organised segregation have been features that have consistently emerged in the debates discussed. These are features that risk impoverishment if confined within a defined 'system', imposed rather than shaped, manufactured rather than grown. Against the 'system' designed as a 'machine' for conformity is the network designed as an organism for growth.

Thirdly, there is the promise of 'openness' as an expression of the need for transparency, lightness, and airiness; more than that, 'closure' is recognised as an unworthy ambition. 'You Are Never Finished' is one of the principles adopted by the Project for Public Spaces for its work on place-making, whose aim is to create environments with a strong sense of community and 'uses that collectively add up to something more than the sum of its often simple parts' (Project for Public Spaces undated). Mae Architects suggest there is value in 'under-designing'; in their view, too much coherence is a constraint—'urbanistically, being too specific can create monocultures' (Mae Architects 2014: 110), and to avoid this there is a need to design with plasticity and flexibility, 'loose fit'. Iteration and renewal are constants, and it is in the ambiguity of uncertain and provisional outcome that meaningful innovation can be achieved. Design that over-prescribes, whether in the urban or domestic setting, in the public or private sphere, is design that forestalls the creative interaction between individual and the common good, between citizen and state, and the possibility of sustainable co-existence between 'strangers'. The aspiration to foreclose is led by excessive ambitions of efficiency and order. The return to 'business as usual' becomes the objective and comfortable reversion to the status quo the only discernible outcome, curtailing options for sustainable change and innovation.

* * *

The broader history of cultural design is a valuable resource for replacing the 'ideal design features' of individual user, system and closure which have been the hallmarks of an administrative justice mentality fallen, inadvertently but not surprisingly, under the sway of law's empire. In community, network and openness are possibilities for the reimagining of administrative justice so that it serves its originating aspirations for social citizenship, a reinvigorated relationship between citizen and state (and indeed between citizen and citizen, and citizen and 'non-citizen'), and active kindness and benevolence in the construction and practice of those relationships. The next two chapters consider the practical application of these concepts to the fabric of administrative justice, and in particular to the distinctive technique of the ombud as the central institution of administrative justice reimagined in the small places of social rights entitlement.

References

Barry, G. (1952). The Festival of Britain 1951. *Journal of the Royal Society of Arts, 100*(4880), 667–704.

Bonsiepe, G. (2010). *Design and Democracy.* London: Bedford Press.

Etherington, Sir Terence, Master of the Rolls. (2017). Lord Slynn Memorial Lecture, June 2017, on Court Estate and Virtual Hearings. Judiciary of England and Wales.

Griffiths, S., & Kippin, H. (2013). Introduction. In H. Kippin et al. (Eds.), *Public Services: A New Reform Agenda.* London: Bloomsbury.

Grindrod, J. (2013). *Concretopia: A Journey around the Rebuilding of Postwar Britain.* Brecon: Old Street Publishing Ltd.

Hanley, L. (2017). *Estates: An Intimate History.* London: Granta.

Harris, A. (2010). *Romantic Moderns: English Writers, Artists and the Imagination from Virginia Woolf to John Piper.* London: Thames & Hudson.

Howard, E. (1965). *Garden Cities of To-Morrow.* Cambridge, MA: MIT Press.

Jackson, A. (2002). From Solving Problems to Selling Product: The Changing Role of Designers in Post-war Britain. Designing Britain 1945–1975. University of Brighton. Retrieved February 18, 2019, from https://vads.ac.uk/learning/designingbritain/html/crd_desref.html

Jacobs, J. (2000). *The Death and Life of Great American Cities.* London: Pimlico.

Mae Architects. (2014). *Places for Strangers: Ideas for Places, People and the City* (S. Bose, Ed.). Zurich: Park Books.

Manzini, E. (2015). *Design, When Everybody Designs: An Introduction to Design for Social Innovation.* Cambridge, MA: MIT Press.

McCarthy, F. (1972). *All Things Bright & Beautiful: Design in Britain 1830 to Today*. London: George Allen & Unwin Ltd.
McCarthy, F. (1982). *British Design Since 1880: A Visual History*. London: Lund Humphries.
McCarthy, F. (2014). *Anarchy & Beauty: William Morris and His Legacy 1960–1960*. London: National Portrait Gallery.
McCormick, M. (2014). Changing Times, Changing Designs: Council Offices Then and Now. *Failed Architecture* blog.
Minton, A. (2012). *Ground Control: Fear and Happiness in the Twenty-First-Century City*. London: Penguin Books.
Mulcahy, L. (2011). *Legal Architecture: Justice, Due Process and the Place of Law*. London: Routledge.
Mussari, M. (2016). *Danish Modern: Between Art and Design*. London: Bloomsbury.
Narkiewicz-Laine, C. (undated). Good Design is a Human Right: An Essay that Commemorates the 65th Anniversary of Good Design. *Chicago Athenaeum Museum of Architecture and Design*.
O'Hara, G. (2008a). The Intellectuals' Ideal: British Views of Scandinavia in the 1950s and 1960s. In J. E. Myhre (Ed.), *Intellectuals in the Public Sphere in Britain and Norway after World War II*. Oslo: Oslo Academic Press.
O'Hara, G. (2008b). Applied Socialism of a Fairy Moderate Kind. *Scandinavian Journal of History, 33*(1), 1–25.
Project for Public Spaces. (undated). Eleven Principles for Creating Great Community Places. *Project for Public Spaces* blog.
Rogers, R. (2017). *A Place for All People*. Edinburgh: Canongate.
Russell, J. (2014). *Peggy Angus: Designer, Teacher, Painter*. Eastbourne: Antiques Collectors' Club/Towner.
Sachs, A. (2007). The South African Experience—Interview with Martin Crick. In *DRC Legal Achievements 2000–2007*. London: Disability Rights Commission.
Sennett, R. (2018). *Building and Dwelling*. London: Allen Lane.
Sossin, L. (2017). Designing Administrative Justice. *Windsor Yearbook of Access to Justice, 34*(1), 87–111.
Terrett, B. (2012a). A Few Notes on Typography. *GDS* Blog.
Terrett, B. (2012b). Ben Terrett on designing GOV.UK. *GDS* Blog.
Tomlinson, J. (2017). The Policy and Politics of Building Tribunals for a Digital Age: How 'Design Thinking' is Shaping the Future of the Public Law System. *UK Constitutional Law* blog.
Woodham, J. M. (1997). *Twentieth-Century Design*. Oxford: Oxford University Press.
Yallop, J. (2015). *Dreamstreets: A Journey through Britain's Village Utopias*. London: Vintage.

CHAPTER 5

Ombud Technique as Demosprudential

Abstract This chapter begins the task of applying the insights drawn from the broader design culture to the reimagining of administrative justice as a means of delivering social rights in the small places of daily life. It does so by concentrating on the ombud institution as the template for administrative justice more generally and by identifying four central aspects of ombud technique: investigation; interpretation; iteration; and institutional focus. In this way, the ombud emerges as 'flaneur', 'story-teller', 'bricoleur' and 'bridge-builder', with a distinctive capacity to give expression to the central demosprudential values of community, network and openness. At the same time the ombud is presented as a demosprudential model for other parts of the reimagined administrative justice fabric.

Keywords Ombud • Technique • Demosprudence • Investigation • Interpretation • Iteration • Institutional focus

The Ombud, Democracy and Human Rights

Consideration of the broader design culture has disclosed an alternative to approaches dominated by the prioritisation of the individual, system and closure, one that seeks to focus instead on values associated with community, network and openness. In the context of administrative justice and

M. Doyle, N. O'Brien, *Reimagining Administrative Justice*,
https://doi.org/10.1007/978-3-030-21388-6_5

human rights, the reimagining entailed by that reprioritisation requires replacing legalism with something more capacious and accommodating to those alternative values.

The ombud in particular is an instructive institution on which to focus our reimagining lens. The distinctiveness of the ombud's technique and the ombud's potential to lend force to social rights without legal enforcement help reunite the apparently separate spheres of administrative justice and human rights. Its occupation of a position between formal adjudication and informal negotiated justice also offers the ombud a potentially pivotal role within the network of institutions that make up the warp and weft of administrative justice: tribunals, courts, regulators, first-instance decision-makers in government departments.

It is in the small places of the state, both national and local, that the public ombud most consistently operates. The Local Government and Social Care Ombudsman (LGSCO), the UK Parliamentary Ombudsman and the Health Services Ombudsman for England (PHSO), the Scottish Public Services Ombudsman (SPSO), the Public Services Ombudsman Wales (PSOW), and the Northern Ireland Public Services Ombudsman (NIPSO) together have jurisdiction over UK government bodies and departments, both central government administrations (in Westminster and in devolved administrations) and all local authorities in the UK, including private sector contractors acting on behalf of the state. Their jurisdiction encompasses the many and varied small places in which decisions are made every day affecting individuals and communities, the essential but unglamorous worlds of education, social care, social security, housing, planning, health care, immigration, waste disposal, and parking. Local authorities in particular are the small places where thousands of decisions on everyday matters are made, and where the potential for democratic participation, for the exercise of community voice, and for the realisation of social rights is most promising.

Local authorities are also the places most severely affected by funding constraints. A report by the National Audit Office in March 2018 on the financial sustainability of local authorities identified the challenges as a combination of cuts by central government (a 28.6% real-term reduction in 'spending power' from government funding and council tax) and an increase in demand for services (National Audit Office 2018a). The unique pressures facing local government, illustrated in a 2018 report by the LGSCO on the funding constraints facing local authorities (LGSCO 2018), make this a particularly salutary arena in which to apply the concepts of community, network and openness in helping to shift administrative justice away from the legal stranglehold in which it has found itself.

The LGSCO also illustrates the democratic context of the ombud's work and how citizen grievance can shape and improve democratic accountability by co-operation with local councillors and Scrutiny Committees. The recommendations made by the LGSCO in its thematic reports include specific questions that councillors might ask local authorities as part of their oversight role, thereby making the ombud a facilitator of ongoing social conversations and of key relationships within the web of a complex accountability network.

Most importantly, and despite the apparent resistance of ombuds in the UK to an explicit human rights role, human rights are widely recognised internationally as the natural habitat of the ombud institution. In seven European states (Albania, Armenia, Azerbaijan, Bosnia and Herzegovina, Poland, Portugal and Spain) the national human rights institution (NHRI, UN status category A) is in fact the national ombud institution (Kucsko-Stadlmayer 2008). In several other states, for example, Hungary, Latvia and Romania, the national ombud institution, although not the NHRI, nevertheless has an explicit human rights mandate (Kucsko-Stadlmayer 2008). In France, the national ombud institution has recently been absorbed within a new human rights institution, the Defenseur des Droits. By contrast, in the UK ombuds do not currently have the status of NHRI and for the most part do not make explicit the implications of human rights in the grievances they investigate, despite human rights, and more specifically social rights, comprising the staple diet of much of their casework (McGregor et al. 2017: 27).

Yet even in the UK, ombuds, no doubt partly in recognition of their own responsibilities as public authorities under the Human Rights Act 1998, have periodically and to a limited extent adopted human rights language in reporting their findings in individual cases. To that extent, the presumption that they are not part of the national human rights structures, even if not formally NHRIs, is open to challenge. For example, in 2008, in a joint investigation of a case involving the inadequate level of care afforded by health and social care services to an adult with severe learning disabilities, the PHSO in her role as Health Service Ombudsman for England and the then Local Government Ombudsman for England (LGO) reported that Articles 3, 8 and 14 of the ECHR were engaged and that both the local authority and health trust had 'neglected to give those issues proper or timely consideration' (LGO and PHSO 2008). The conclusion, although in no way pretending to be a formal determination of human rights liability, nevertheless followed that this omission was so significant that it amounted to maladministration and contributed to the injustice suffered.

Similar conclusions have arisen in a handful of other reports by UK public-sector ombuds: for example, another joint finding by the Health Service Ombudsman and the Local Government Ombudsman (LGO) (as it was known at that time) that in six unrelated cases local authorities and NHS trusts had failed to give expression to 'human rights principles' and a 'human rights culture' in the way they treated patients with severe learning disabilities (LGO and PHSO 2009); separate findings by the LGO that a council failed to give adequate attention to its obligations under Article 8 when handling confidential data relating to a family of travellers (LGO 2008) and that in another case local social services failed to consider an elderly disabled woman's human rights when assessing her housing needs (LGO, Report on an investigation into complaint No. 06/A/10428 against the London Borough of Havering, 31 October 2007); and two findings by the SPSO, that dignity and privacy were 'denied' by a hospital in its care of an elderly patient with dementia, and that the HRA had not been taken into account by a local authority when assessing the transport needs of disabled students (SPSO, Ombudsman's Commentary, May 2006 Reports; O'Brien 2009; O'Brien and Thompson 2010).

These few examples (all of which, tellingly, relate to health and social care, arguably more readily identifiable as ones to raise human rights issues) are a natural extension of the public sector ombud's primary function of 'humanising the bureaucracy'; the willingness to resort to human rights language demonstrates an intention to add weight to the findings made in a particular case and so express a measure of moral indignation that might otherwise be obscured by the conventional language of maladministration. By interpreting bureaucratic failure in human rights terms, the ombud is able to draw out more vividly the human cost and so reflect something of the subjective force that infused the complaint.

Modern Ombudsman Practice and the Marginalisation of the Ombud

Notwithstanding occasional human rights flourishes of this sort, the public ombuds in the UK have been more often noticeable for their absence from public debate about human rights issues that fall within their respective spheres of influence. In 2014, in an evaluation of the impact of the LGSCO's work, the authors predicted 'stagnation' if ombuds remain unwilling to engage in 'radical thinking' and contemplate a fresh approach 'grounded in contemporary notions of the public good'. Failing that, they argued, the institutions of administrative justice, including the ombud, would 'become increasingly less and less relevant to the needs of the day' (Kirkham and Martin 2014).

That prediction has turned out to be accurate, as evidenced by the absence of the ombuds from public debate in the wake of major events such as the fire at Grenfell Tower (the subject of a public inquiry) and the Home Office's treatment of the Windrush generation (National Audit Office 2018b). That the Housing Ombudsman and the Parliamentary Ombudsman have not been mentioned in the context of either is a telling indicator of their marginalisation. On the other hand, that the LGSCO has had a voice in debates about local authority funding cuts, especially in the context of social care and special educational needs, is indicative of more promising potential.

That potential arises from a willingness to adopt a particular conception of the relationship between the individual and the state and of the role of the ombud in 'mediating' that relationship. The typical prioritisation of individualized complaint mechanisms, whether of ombud or court-based provenance, creates a strong polarization between individual and state, with very little in between. By contrast, an alternative approach would deliberately evoke a more 'complex' social space, in which the full range of civil society is acknowledged and credited with an emancipative role that is egalitarian, not just libertarian. The ombud then emerges as a potential catalyst of civil society, energising those intermediate institutions that comprise the complex social space between state and individual and that can more effectively co-ordinate and implement local initiatives on the ground to hold the state to account against its equality, and thereby social rights, commitments.

In the UK, however, the recognition of Modern Ombudsman Practice as an agreed set of desirable characteristics appears to have settled for the time being any debate about the future direction of the ombud. The recent Report of the Independent Peer Review of the Parliamentary and Health Service Ombudsman (PHSO) entitled the *Value for Money Study* (Tyndall et al. 2018), for example, takes Modern Ombudsman Practice as the assumed shared ambition. Modern Ombudsman Practice in this context discloses a consistent value system comprising effective and efficient service, stakeholder evaluation, robust management systems, quality assurance, easier public access, flexible and speedy dispute resolution, professional accreditation and public accountability. The chief values of efficiency, effectiveness and economy, with a strong emphasis on the priority of the individual user, on system and the need for proportionate dispute resolution, are also those of the New Public Management (Drewry 2009). Modern Ombudsman Practice shares those values and is therefore constitutive of what has been described as the 'managerial ombudsman' (Gill et al. 2019).

Despite the ambitions of Modern Ombudsman Practice to demonstrate efficiency and effectiveness and to deliver resolution that allows for a return to business as usual, much current ombuds practice in the UK resembles that involved in producing a digital film, a task primarily focused on 'post-production'. Ombuds come late to the party; the main work is therefore in piecing together and editing the digital footage after the event. In contrast, analogue filmmaking, where the work takes place in the moment and is guided by human intervention and decision-making, might provide a better metaphor for a demosprudential ombud. Analogue filmmaking is often derided as an outdated technology that prohibits the scope for manipulation and enhancement that digital provides—it is the old Technicolor to today's computer-generated imagery (CGI). But the richness of both the process and the final result it produces have been celebrated by artists who argue that in ditching the 'old' technology we lose something in the relationship it fostered between filmmaker, film and audience. Film director Christopher Nolan talks of the serendipity of analogue versus digital in film, of the uncertainty; not everything is in the control of the filmmaker, mistakes happen, but there is in film, more than in digital formats, greater possibility. The difference between digital and analogue filmmaking is in the process, as artist Tacita Dean points out: 'Digital relies on post-production. No longer do you rely on the moment; and you lose a certain vitality of the moment' (Higgins 2011). Dean acknowledges that digital is 'a great enabler of immediacy, reproduction and convenience', but it lacks the ability to 'create poetry'; 'it neither breathes nor wobbles, but tidies up our society, correcting it, and then leaves no trace' (Eakin 2011). Ombuds in the UK are for the most part stuck in post-production, making them less able to identify concerns early on and to hear and act on the murmurs that circulate as problems arise, as in Grenfell and the Windrush human rights tragedies.

The focus on resolution arguably has contributed to this marginalisation of the ombud. The procedural flexibility of informal resolution, adopted increasingly by ombuds in the UK since the 1990s, is at odds with the ombud's function to promote high administrative standards, which might be best served through statutory investigations rather than grievance-settlement. More widely, questions arise as to whether a resolution focus is appropriate in the context of complaints that arise in public law and administrative justice and in light of procedural reform in tribunals, and specifically a shift away from oral hearings: 'When a citizen asserts an entitlement which a public agency denies, should the redress system seek to resolve the dispute through negotiation or mediation to the satisfaction of the parties, or should it restrict itself to upholding the entitlement when it is made out and to denying it when it is not?' (Richardson and Genn 2007: 133).

Legal Enforcement or 'Giving Force' to Social Rights?

The marginalisation in the UK of ombuds from human rights discourse has occurred as a result of the emphasis on legality, despite the continuing debate about the justiciability of social rights in particular. As previously observed, the original integration of civil and social rights within the Universal Declaration of 1948 quickly gave way to formal division underpinned by different modes of enforcement. Whilst civil rights have consistently conformed to expectations of judicial enforcement, social rights have been left to alternatives that lack the perceived gravity of enforceable legal adjudication. In Europe, for example, human rights are far more likely to be associated with the civil instrument of the European Convention and its enforcement mechanism the European Court of Human Rights in Strasbourg than with the Social Charter and the Council of Europe Committee of Social Rights as the means of giving force, short of enforceability, to its very different content.

Far from celebrating the alternative mechanisms for giving force to social rights, the advocates of social rights have often lamented the lack of legal enforcement and argued for ways of making social rights part of the constitution and in that way justiciable in the courts. However, even when the desirability of process pluralism is conceded, a principle of co-ordination between the different parts of the accountability system has given priority to the courts as the leading protagonist in any future partnership of relevant agencies. Informal mechanisms, such as the ombud or mediation, or even tribunals, have as a result found themselves relegated to the margins and denigrated as not really up to the job of providing effective accountability for social rights violations (King 2012).

It is argued, for example, that such informal mechanisms lack general jurisdiction and so are unable to apply legal principles in a way that ensures system-wide consistency. Tribunals and ombuds in particular are accused of making less use of participatory features, such as third-party intervention in proceedings or relaxation of rules of standing to extend the potential range of protagonists in grievance procedures. Ombuds are deemed to lack an effective publicity function and as a result are thought to have only a diminished expressive role in articulating norms and building up a corpus of authoritative precedent as an instrument of constitutional authority. Resistant to adversarialism as a means of eliciting evidence, the ombud, with its essentially inquisitorial investigative process, is criticised for reducing the individual antagonist's ability to build her own case and, because traditionally concerned with maladministration rather than substantive illegality, considered no substitute for constitutional legal accountability (King 2012). The negative conclusion inevitably follows: 'one rarely bargains in the shadow of an ombudsman report' (King 2012: 93).

The suspicion endures in the UK that the ombud in particular, and administrative justice in general, is a pale imitation of authentic justiciability in respect of social and relational rights. Such critiques of the ombud and of administrative justice are prefaced by the assumption that legalism is the best we can hope for when responding to citizen grievance. That assumption is open to challenge, however. Looking back, we see that in their social democratic origins both human rights and administrative justice aspired to extra-legality as the means of embedding more humane values in the public realm before being captured by New Public Management and neoliberal priorities. We also see that design more broadly was similarly captured by the problematic and ultimately limiting concepts of individual, system and closure, and also that design culture offers progressive alternatives to these as means of expressing democratic principle in the construction of the social and cultural environment. The ombud, as the chief battleground in administrative justice and human rights for the competing claims of adjudication and mediation, warrants closer scrutiny as a potential template for these wider alternative approaches.

Examining the distinctive characteristics of the ombud makes it possible to construct a stronger image of how it can uniquely reinforce the prioritisation of community, network and openness and so reconnect administrative justice with the values of democracy and human rights. These characteristics are reflected in ombuds' techniques that prioritise 'a different mode' of sensing, one that is 'tentative, tempting, reflexive and uncertain' (Pavoni et al. 2018: 7). This sensory mode, adopting sight, sound and touch, works particularly well with administrative justice because of its immediacy and its everyday reach: 'We relate to, and encounter, the State in many different ways all the time. ... Indeed, in so far as the State regulates the quality of the air we breathe, the water we drink, the landscapes and the townscapes we inhabit, we might be said to be touching it every minute of our lives' (Design Council 2004: 8). Touch is also the only sense that is reflexive; you cannot touch someone without being touched (Cole 2016: 174). Techniques that employ the senses counter the perceived 'untouchability' of the state and have the potential to transform and humanise the everyday encounters that make up the world of administrative justice and social rights.

Investigation—The Ombud as Flaneur/Flaneuse

Central to ombud-technique, and chief among its claims to offer a viable alternative to adjudication or to mediation as a form of negotiated justice, is the practice of investigation. When the Parliamentary Commissioner Act gave effect to the ombud institution in the UK for the first time in 1967 it granted to the ombud the function of investigating grievances and very little else. It was not the role of the ombud either to adjudicate or mediate but quite simply to investigate, to report on the investigation and to make a recommendation, if she thought necessary. There was no explicit power to make formal findings or provide a remedy for an individual citizen. The very practice of investigation was in itself a form of remedy, a means of clearing the air, shining a light in the dark corners of official administration.

When the ombud was first introduced in Scandinavia, this investigative function also took centre stage. In that case, the residual power of individual citizens to exercise the right to freedom of information was in the case of the ombud writ large and generalised so that the ombud in effect stood in the shoes of the individual citizen and on behalf of the community exercised the right to freedom of information so that what had previously been hidden was now made manifest and open to public gaze. It was the ability of the Scandinavian ombud to 'glimpse behind the scenes' of executive action, as the Danish Ombudsman put it (Hurwitz 1960), that prompted the creation of the office in the first place (Busck 1995; Holm 1995).

The centrality of investigation to the work of the ombud is further reflected in the fact that most ombuds, at least outside the UK, have the ability to commence an investigation even without a particular grievance being referred to them by an individual citizen. The availability of this 'own initiative' or 'public value' investigative power enables the ombud to keep her ear to the ground, to listen out for legitimate grievance, especially on the part of those who might not easily make a formal complaint in person, and to conduct an investigation, so bringing to light for deliberation those circumstances that might otherwise have remained hidden from public view. It is revealing in this regard that in Portuguese 'ombud' is sometimes translated as *ouvidoria* (the auditor or listener), evoking the centrality of this listening function.

Not just listening, but looking also, is an instructive metaphor for this investigative function as central to the ombud technique. In the context of the law, sight is considered a deficit compromising impartiality, but this image of justice as blindfolded is a relatively recent creation. Before the sixteenth century, sight was considered to be 'essential for justice to manage well the sword and the scale… "the eye of the law" or the "eye of justice"—alert and controlling—was an image of great symbolic value' (Franca 2018: 171). In the context of urban design, the notion of looking evokes the human perspective in the cityscape, the need not for the bird's-eye view of a New York skyscraper, but for the view from the street-level of a Parisian boulevard (de Certeau 1984). When combined with the ability to seek out grievance using the licence of an own-initiative investigatory power, the metaphor of looking elides into that of the urban explorer, or *flaneur/flaneuse*, and of the practice of *flanerie* as a quintessentially modern and democratic practice, transgressive of boundaries, 'restoring the primacy of the street', available to all, and unpredictable in its invitations. The ombud, rather than being positioned at the apex of a 'superescalated' complaints pyramid, should instead be positioned at the base—not necessarily for the function of investigating complaints as they arise, but in feeling the ground out of which complaints percolate. *Flanerie* in this sense is more than aimless wandering; it is instead a means of sensing texture first-hand, of making connections that might otherwise evade observation (Elkin 2016; Solnit 2002). The urban walker, exemplified by the *flaneur/flaneuse*, is a keen and curious observer. In a similar way, the investigative technique of the ombud entails a process of observation and exploration, questioning, listening and looking. The ombud's path, like that of the *flaneur/flaneuse*, is unpredictable but cognisant nonetheless of basic norms and procedural safeguards: the prudent *flaneur/flaneuse* does not, after all, walk in front of a bus.

Procedural safeguards rather than rules and barriers are the key to the urban design concept of Shared Space. Developed in the 1970s by Dutch engineer Hans Monderman, Shared Space removes traditional safety elements intended to control traffic and separate pedestrians from vehicles—kerbs, crossings, traffic lights, railings—in a counterintuitive attempt to improve safety. What Monderman observed was that these safety elements prevent road users from interacting with each other; when lines are blurred between street and pavement, users are forced to look, engage and negotiate with one another, eye to eye. Studies of the more than 100 shared spaces Monderman created in the Netherlands show a reduction in accidents and no fatalities (Toth 2009).

Shared Space is a political concept as much as an engineering one, and a way of thinking as much as a design issue (Toth 2009). Politicians and planners are forced to do more than approve plans (indeed it is in some ways anti-plan); they must make decisions about the level of civic participation and the degree to which civic buy-in can be fostered by the design process. The success of Shared Space depends on people's willingness to trust strangers, the most political of issues and the foundation of democracy (Solnit 2002: 218). Prioritising the skill of looking, and recasting the ombud as *flaneur/flanuese*, therefore offers up potential for democratic participation and co-design of investigation in the sense of Manzini's design for social innovation.

Embracing the unknown and unexpected, observing procedural safeguards rather than following rigid rules, has a parallel in photography. As art historian Teju Cole writes of photojournalism, novices often refer to mathematical formulae or rules of composition (such as the 'rule of thirds' and the 'golden ratio')—codes to help us in our looking. The reality, he writes, 'is that there is usually a much more improvisatory and flexible mathematical order at play in a successful photograph' (Cole 2016: 163). There is an uncertainty, an element of chance, and no right answer. Yet despite the improvisational nature of the process of photographing, despite the photographer not being in control of everything in the scene, in the resulting photo 'everything is in its right place' ('right' as in aesthetically pleasing ratios, relationships and repetitions), a result of both chance (luck) and skill (intuition). Investigation, similarly, makes use of both chance and skill. It is something different from either adjudication or mediation and is frequently relegated as a mere step on the way to the finality of either or both. In the case of the ombud, like that of the *flaneur/flaneuse*, investigation is an end in itself, but an end that when coupled with other practices is also the beginning of a conversation that is without a prescribed or pre-determined destination. In the case of the ombud, those other practices include the skills of story-telling, bricolage, and bridge-building.

Interpretation—The Ombud as Story-Teller

A complement to investigation is the skill of story-telling, of narrative interpretation, of making sense of what the ombud sees and hears. In its classic form, the ombud does not just investigate but also 'reports' on what she discovers. In this regard, the ombud has the benefit of being a repeat-player, a role-literate participant whose experience and expertise enable her to detect patterns and so invest meaning in what might to the individual citizen appear random and isolated circumstances.

In doing so, a demosprudential ombud adopts active listening, a skill employed by mediators to encourage story-telling as a way to identify the interests that are often unseen but that shape people's response to conflict. State institutions, and the decision-makers or street-level bureaucrats who operate in them, tend not to adopt active listening but a more focused listening with purpose, a necessarily selective type of listening that aims to get at the nub of the problem and closer therefore to a solution that fits within bureaucratic constraints. Active listening, in contrast, is more akin to *flaneusing* in that there is no fixed destination; to listen actively requires becoming 'sensitised to the ways in which real people tell their stories and express their fears and desires. For most people, life is recorded in fragmented narrative rather than coherent speeches, and in heartfelt values rather than ideological stances' (Coleman 2004: 44). Narrative interpretation that results from active listening ensures that a range of interests, not only those that appear on the face of a complaint or that fit with definitions of poor administration, are brought to the surface.

The skill of narrative interpretation is different from the task of decision-making and from the ambition of problem-solving. The ombud is not in a position to pronounce enforceable judgments like a court. Instead, she offers persuasive interpretations that must command respect, trust and credibility. The ombud has a mandate of influence not sanction, and her word, although authoritative, is not necessarily the last word. To that extent, the ombud is engaged in an exercise that is inherently inconclusive and open-ended, ill-equipped to achieve closure or resolution. In order to command that credibility, the ombud, more than a court, must carry her audience with her. The challenge is more than merely resolving a dispute or solving a problem and instead that of making sense in a way that depends on a viable relationship between the ombud and the parties concerned, and between the parties themselves.

Interpretative activity of this sort is a user-centred approach but one that prioritises connectivity and focuses on the community of users, not single individuals. Interpretation is in this way a form of social conversation, multifaceted and multi-dimensional, in which different actors participate in different ways and at different times. This essentially collaborative and co-operative activity is a means of ensuring not only that a problem is solved but that the solution has social meaning. Such participatory engagement is in effect 'the only way of making sure that the technical solution found will actually be culturally and socially acceptable to the people and communities it is to benefit' (Manzini 2015: 45).

Iteration—The Ombud as *Bricoleur*

Closely linked to this style of interpretative sense-making are two other characteristics of the ombud technique: its iterative process and its institutional focus. The ombud technique is necessarily iterative since it relies on the piecemeal accumulation that goes with the inquisitorial mode of fact-finding. Instead of a one-off trial or tribunal hearing, the ombud's involvement is occasional and incremental. The to-and-fro of ombud engagement with the parties entails that, as part of the rolling process of interpretation, there is scope for sharing provisional assessments, for pausing to take stock, review and revise, for asking direct questions, sharing points of view, encouraging open and continuing dialogue between the parties, not as a matter of interest-bargaining, as might be the case in a trial, but as a process of public reasoning and deliberation. The ombud's gaze is not wholly distracted by the episodic; her job is not finished at some determinate point but potentially open-ended and subject to revision. There is, for example, scope for the ombud to widen the original investigation, follow-up on recommendations, develop thematic perspectives and embark upon broader educational and directive tasks.

This style of iteration allows for a measure of 'free-flow'. Its focus on openness, like the concept of Shared Spaces for improved safety and traffic flow, is the opposite of what design theorists call 'closed' design, for example in the 'funnels' of some 1960s housing estates, whose walkways and subways direct pedestrians and prohibit meandering or wandering, instead channelling 'pedestrians from home to shop and back as a funnel directs liquid into a bottle' (Hanley 2017: 125). Funnels make for closure, for impermeable boundaries and predictability. Iteration, by contrast, facilitates the exercise of discretion in response to changing circumstance, including the changing context of a grievance as it progresses through the investigatory process.

This resistance to closure is not dreamy or idealistic but relentlessly realistic, not least because of the unlikelihood of achieving anything like complete 'user satisfaction' at the end. On the contrary, closure or resolution prematurely shuts down expansive conversation and future collaboration and so becomes a 'point of no return' (Fredman 2008: 149). The aim is not so much to reach a destination, as in the creation of a 'product', but to facilitate a sustainable relationship, to move seamlessly back and forth, to test out provisional landings, gaining insights and information along the way. Sennett describes the 'turning points' that change the direction of informal conversation, taking tangents; like the woodworker responding to knots and grain in the wood, 'At each stage, something occurs which changes the work he set out to do' (Sennett 2018: 195–196). An iterative technique embraces the informal turning points of a conversation and if necessary goes off at tangents that may prove more important than the grievance as originally, and partially, articulated (Manzini 2015; Sennett 2018).

Such a technique also allows for equal voices to emerge, reflecting the democratic underpinnings of Manzini's design for social innovation, in which expert and non-expert designers work together to take responsibility for the design process—such that it should be difficult, he says, to identify who did what. Manzini cites the initiatives of democratic psychiatry, developed by Italian psychiatrist Franco Busaglia in the 1970s, as an example of designing for social innovation in practice. Busaglia's democratic psychiatry movement adopted a capabilities approach as a way to enable mental health patients to engage in fulfilling (and sometimes economically rewarding) activities—to take them out of the asylum and into the community, running restaurants and other commercial enterprises. Designing in this way is not neat and tidy; it is, instead, 'an inextricable tangle', but one bursting with creativity and the potential 'to imagine feasible solutions and create the conditions to tap the social energy available' (Manzini 2015: 62).

The ombud's mode is to that extent not so much that of engineering but of *bricolage*, of trial and error and putting to creative use whatever comes to hand rather than sticking doggedly to some preconceived and strategic direction (Levi-Strauss 1966). Unlike the systematic and scientific engineer, the ombud as *bricoleur* is suspicious of holistic and totalising system and of permanent closure. Her conclusions are inherently provisional, revisable and deliberative. The true ombud persuades but does not compel.

Institutional Focus—The Ombud as Bridge-Builder

Finally, an important aspect of the ombud-alternative to the judicial process lies in its ability to look beyond an individual grievance to the underlying relational deficit that gave rise to the grievance and that awaits restoration. Whereas the judicial process is singular in its episodic gaze, the ombud has scope to draw upon the intelligence yielded from citizen grievance, detect underlying patterns, and nudge the parties towards restorative outcomes that carry with them a measure of public value rather than immediate and short-term individual redress. In that way, the focus of the ombud is inherently communitarian, not individualistic. As the development of the influential Danish model of the ombud indicates, any focus on the conduct of individual officials quickly gave way in the 1960s to concern about the institutional environment that had nurtured the breakdown of relationship between the citizen and the state at street-level. The reform of institutions rather than the chastisement of individuals emerged as the main focus of the ombud's work, the purification of whatever had become rotten in the state of Denmark its overriding objective.

In this way, the ombud is drawn to the task of building bridges between citizen and state, between communities of experience and institutions. Collaboration and co-operation entail skill in the craft of working together 'as an exchange in which the participants benefit from the encounter' (Manzini 2015: 93). The aim, however, is not the restoration of personal ties between individuals but the restoration of bridges between citizens and their representative institutions. The ombud is in effect a bridge-builder who keeps open the highways and byways of the democratic state and prevents its arterial roads from becoming fatally congested.

In French-speaking jurisdictions, the concept of ombud is translated by the term *mediateur*. For English-speakers, *mediateur* carries with it overtones of mediation as a form of dispute resolution. The French invokes something more ambitious, to do with the ombud as an intermediary, a facilitator, a builder or restorer of bridges that have become damaged and rendered untrustworthy. Recent empirical research (Creutzfeldt 2016) has demonstrated the critical importance of trust between ombud and citizen but also between citizens and their institutions, and of the role of the ombud in restoring trust as its primary remedial function. For the ombud, mediation in this sense is therefore more than mere dispute resolution or the creation of a safe space for competitive interest-bargaining between antagonistic combatants, for a form of negotiated justice. Mediation for the ombud, or *mediateur*, is a technique for allowing citizens' voices to be heard, for constructing bridge-building dialogue and for the restoration of relationships that are public and institutional rather than private and personal.

* * *

The characterisation in this chapter of the ombud's technique has drawn on wider design culture to illustrate how the distinctive characteristics of investigation set it apart from adjudication, on the one hand, and mediation on the other. In adopting investigation as the primary tool of its work, the ombud rejects a focus on the 'atomised' user as victim, on boundaried system, and on the resignation of closure. Instead, in prioritising community, flexible network and open-ended investigation, the ombud reconnects administrative justice with the values of democracy and human rights. In particular, this characterisation of ombud technique has helped identify features that, when put into practice, might yet achieve the reconnection between administrative justice and social rights that the reimagining proposed by this book requires.

The next chapter, drawing on examples both within and beyond the UK, begins to explore how the use of such techniques may serve a broader demosprudential vision for the administrative justice fabric as a whole.

References

Busck, L. (1995). The History and Development of the Institution of Ombudsman. In H. Gammeltoft-Hansen (Ed.), *The Danish Ombudsman*. Copenhagen: The Danish Ombudsman.

Cole, T. (2016). *Known and Strange Things*. London: Faber & Faber.

Coleman, S. (2004). Tangible Democracy. In *Touching the State: What Does It Mean to Be a Citizen in the 21st Century?* London: Design Council and Institute for Public Policy Research.

Creutzfeldt, N. (2016). A Voice for Change? Trust Relationships between Ombudsmen, Individuals and Public Service Providers. *Journal of Social Welfare and Family Law, 38*, 460–479.

de Certeau, M. (1984). *The Practice of Everyday Life*. Berkeley: University of California Press.

Design Council. (2004). *Touching the State: What Does It Mean to Be a Citizen in the 21st Century?* London: Design Council and Institute for Public Policy Research.

Drewry, G. (2009). The Judicialisation of 'Administrative' Tribunals in the UK: From Hewart to Legatt. *Transylvanian Review of Administrative Sciences, 28*, 45–64.

Eakin, E. (2011, October 31). Celluloid Hero. *The New Yorker*.

Elkin, L. (2016). *Flaneuse: Women Walk the City in Paris, New York, Tokyo, Venice and London*. London: Vintage.

Franca, M. (2018). The Blindness of Justice: An Iconographic Dialogue between Art and Law. In A. Pavoni et al. (Eds.), *Law and the Senses: See*. London: University of Westminster Press.

Fredman, S. (2008). *Human Rights Transformed: Positive Rights and Positive Duties*. Oxford: OUP.

Gill, C., Mullen, T., & Vivian, N. (2019). *The Managerial Ombuds* (forthcoming).

Hanley, L. (2017). *Estates: An Intimate History*. London: Granta.

Higgins, C. (2011, October 10). Tacita Dean's Turbine Hall Film Pays Homage to a Dying Medium. *The Guardian*.

Holm, N. E. (1995). The Ombudsman—A Gift from Scandinavia to the World. In H. Gammeltoft-Hansen (Ed.), *The Danish Ombudsman*. Copenhagen: The Danish Ombudsman.

Hurwitz, S. (1960, May 12). Interview with H W R Wade and J A G Griffiths. *The Listener*.

King, J. (2012). *Judging Social Rights*. Cambridge: CUP.

Kirkham, R., & Martin, J. (2014). Designing an English Public Services Ombudsman. *Journal of Social Welfare and Family Law, 36*(3), 330–448.

Kucsko-Stadlmayer, G. (Ed.). (2008). *European Ombudsman-Institutions*. Vienna: Springer.

Levi-Strauss, C. (1966). *The Savage Mind*. Chicago: Chicago University Press.
Local Government Ombudsman (LGO). (2008). *Report on an Investigation into Complaint Nos 06/A/16993, 06/A/16997 and 06/A/17360 against Basildon District Council*. London: LGO.
Local Government Ombudsman and Parliamentary and Health Service Ombudsman (LGO and PHSO). (2008). *Injustice in Residential Care: A Joint Report by the Local Government Ombudsman and Health Service Ombudsman for England*. HC Paper No. 421, Session 2007/08. London: The Stationery Office.
Local Government Ombudsman and Parliamentary and Health Service Ombudsman (LGO and PHSO). (2009). *Six Lives: The Provision of Public Services to People with Learning Disabilities*. HC Paper No. 203, Session 2008/09. London: The Stationery Office.
Local Government and Social Care Ombudsman (LGSCO). (2018). *Under Pressure—The Impact of the Changing Environment on Local Government Complaints*. London: LGSCO.
Manzini, E. (2015). *Design, When Everybody Designs: An Introduction to Design for Social Innovation*. Cambridge, MA: MIT Press.
McGregor, et al. (2017). *National Human Rights Institutions in Europe and dispute Resolution: A Mapping*. Oxford Brookes University, University of Essex and University of Bristol.
National Audit Office. (2018a). *Comptroller and Auditor General, Financial Sustainability of Local Authorities 2018*. HC 834 Session 2017–2019. London: National Audit Office.
National Audit Office. (2018b). *Handling of the Windrush Situation*. HC 1622 Session 2017–2019. London: National Audit Office.
O'Brien, N. (2009, July). Ombudsmen and Social Rights Adjudication. *Public Law*, pp. 466–478.
O'Brien, N., & Thompson, B. (2010). Human Rights Accountability in the UK: Deliberative Democracy and the Role of the Ombudsman. *European Human Rights Law Review*, *5*, 504–512.
Pavoni, A., et al. (Eds.). (2018). *Law and the Senses: See*. London: University of Westminster Press.
Richardson, G., & Genn, H. (2007, January). Tribunals in Transition: Resolution or Adjudication? *Public Law*, pp. 116–141.
Sennett, R. (2018). *Building and Dwelling*. London: Allen Lane.
Solnit, R. (2002). *Wanderlust: A History of Walking*. London: Granta.
Toth, G. (2009). Where the Sidewalk Doesn't End. *Project for Public Spaces* blog.
Tyndall, P., Mitchell, C., & Gill, C. (2018). *Value for Money*. London: PHSO.

CHAPTER 6

The Demosprudential Ombud in Practice

Abstract This chapter turns from theory to practice by considering ways in which response to citizen grievance, whether by progressive judicial intervention or ombud practice, has already begun to conform to demosprudential values. In particular, the chapter considers public interest litigation in India, the operation of the ombud in Argentina as a 'horizontal accountability mechanism' and of the ombud in Greece as an instrument of equality and non-discrimination, and the systemic interventions of public-sector ombuds in the UK. The chapter also identifies the importance of mediation, of an ethic of care and of compassion as means of giving full expression to the values of community, network and openness.

Keywords Demosprudence • Public interest litigation • Horizontal accountability mechanism • Mediation

Demosprudence in Theory and Practice

The previous chapter's characterisation of the ombud technique as marked by investigation, interpretation, iteration and institutional focus already indicates ways in which the ombud is uniquely placed to be receptive to the alternative values to legalism represented by community, network and openness. The metaphors of *flaneur/flaneuse*, story-teller, *bricoleur* and bridge-builder further serve to accentuate those tendencies inherent in the institutional identity of the ombud. These are characteristics that distance

M. Doyle, N. O'Brien, *Reimagining Administrative Justice*,
https://doi.org/10.1007/978-3-030-21388-6_6

the ombud from the mode of adjudication adopted by judicial institutions and their imitators. They also distance the ombud, however, from the alternative of mediation when it in turn is reduced merely to a form of dispute resolution underpinned by the assumptions of legalism.

In order to gauge how the ombud might build in practice on its inherently alternative characteristics, it is instructive to consider the ways in which ombuds and indeed courts dealing with social rights issues have already begun to develop approaches that hint at the sort of reimagining that is necessary if the values of community, network and openness are to take pride of place. In this way, the ombud can begin to fulfil its alternative potential and thereby serve as a template for the reimagining of administrative justice more generally, and especially in its relationship with the human rights of small places. The overarching approach that can accommodate these developments can best be described as 'demosprudential'.

'Demosprudence' is a term intended to denote practices that build on the ability of social movements or mobilized communities to make, interpret and change the law. It is a means of making more democratic the process of responding to citizen grievance and of ensuring that legal change is embedded in broader cultural transformation. It is a departure therefore from those more familiar forms of legal liberalism based on a common law mentality of strict legal precedent, enforcement, adversarialism and individualism; and from the unwavering separation of law from ethics, culture and politics.

Demosprudence, despite its democratic credentials, values privileged 'role literate participants', who can serve as focal points for articulating grievance and in that way help 'ground and frame the discourse' (Guinier 2013). The demosprudential literature offers as a prime example the dissenting judge, who gives expression to democratic perspectives whilst being in the judicial minority (Ray 2011; Guinier 2013; Guinier and Torres 2014). It is not hard to imagine how an ombud might even more readily fit that role.

Demosprudence is, more specifically, a theory of law that seeks to democratise the process of responding to grievance by fashioning values and processes that can enable civic participation and create bridges between different interests. It is consistent with, but not limited to, related ideas such as public interest law, network governance, democratic experimentalism, legal pragmatism, deliberative democracy, therapeutic justice and problem-solving courts. It is a theory of law that also lends itself to application in the context of the ombud conceived as Tribune of the

People, People's Defender, Mediateur, or Defensoria del Pueblo. It is less obviously at home, perhaps, in an institution construed as Parliamentary Commissioner for Administration, Health Service Commissioner or Commissioner for Local Administration, although calls even in the UK for 'a People's Ombudsman' have obvious resonance.

The literature of legal pragmatism and deliberative problem-solving provides useful underpinning for such democratic engagement in the process of responding to citizen grievance (Simon 2004, 2009; Klein 2007; Sabel and Simon 2004; Chayes 1976; Menkel-Meadow 2004/2005, 2006; Gutmann and Thompson 2004; Dorf and Sabel 1998; Berman and Feinblatt 2001; Hertogh 2001). Instead of prioritising individual victims, such approaches emphasise citizen empowerment and the common good; flexible principles, rather than strict rules, as normative standards; deliberation and public reasoning instead of adversarialism and command-and-control methods of enforcement; an iterative process and revisable opinions instead of closure and final resolution.

This theoretical perspective provides the basis for a very different approach from adversarial and individualistic legalism to the task of responding to citizen grievance. It is an approach that has already been put into practice in the context of network governance, responsive regulation, and democratic experimentalism. Such approaches discount top-down or hierarchical prescription of rules which are then subject to retrospective sanction. Instead of this command-and-control framework, they aim for a more participatory and collaborative approach, in which multiple stakeholders co-operate to achieve a common purpose. The process that underpins such approaches is, in contrast to the set menu of proceduralism, a more experimental and deliberative *a la carte* suite of options that enables citizens to acquire the information necessary to hold institutions to account themselves, without recourse to centralised command-and-control agencies, such as conventional courts. In this context, even 'judging' becomes a form of nudging, to give force to shared values and principles, rather than enforcement of prescribed rules (Klein 2007; Dorf and Sabel 1998; Sabel and Simon 2004).

India: Public Interest Litigation

The translation of these more deliberative and experimental approaches into problem-solving courts has encouraged the prospect of better outcomes for the parties to a dispute as well as more public benefit for broader communities, for example in the development of community courts as a model for deliberation on domestic violence and mental health issues in the US (Berman and Feinblatt 2001). In other contexts, the courts themselves have effectively been restructured, demosprudentially, to enable not just public interest litigation but a more democratically authentic process for addressing social rights disputes in a forum that is both deliberative and democratic, notably in India and South Africa (Fredman 2008).

In the world's largest and most diverse democracy, India, for example, the realisation of social rights entitlement has depended since Independence in 1947 upon the gradual, and partial, transformation of the Indian courts from scenes of adversarial procedure into a forum which is cooperative, where proceedings are conducted in the public interest and are frequently demosprudential. As the Supreme Court emphasised as long ago as 1986, such public interest litigation is 'not litigation of an adversary character for the purpose of holding the State…responsible for making reparation, but it is a public interest litigation which involves a collaborative and cooperative effort…for the purpose of making human rights meaningful for the weaker sections of the community' (Fredman 2008: 127).

That cooperative effort, or 'judicial conversation', has entailed in India the abolition of the victim test, so that the right to bring cases has been extended beyond the especially vulnerable individuals of limited resource who might be the primary 'victims' of deprivation; the appointment by the courts of special commissioners to do some of the 'own initiative' fact-finding; the enlargement of judicial remedy to range beyond the redress of individual wrongs to broader institutional issues and the monitoring of any such remedies proposed; and, perhaps most importantly, the inauguration, at least in principle, of a model of adjudication that is deliberative rather than rooted in ultimately divisive interest-bargaining (Fredman 2008).

As a result, the judiciary has had to reformulate its role in public interest cases by abandoning its 'command and control' methods and instead becoming 'an ally to strong civil society groups and movements in their attempt to make the processes of Indian democracy more participatory, inclusive and effective in pursuing the development goals enshrined in the Constitution' (Khilnani et al. 2012: 367). The successes of this approach have included reinforcement of the civil and political rights of prisoners, the rights of those detained in mental hospitals, and the rights of victims of crime, as well as transformational 'right to food' decisions, which have provided a cooked mid-day meal for up to 10 million schoolchildren. The extensive litigation about mental patients is especially significant since it has not merely imposed negative duties of restraint on the state preventing the routine imprisonment of the mentally disabled, but comprehensive positive duties, including the construction of a better resourced psychiatric hospital and the access to pensions for those with mental disabilities (Fredman 2008).

The Ombud as 'Horizontal Accountability Mechanism'

Elsewhere, the ombud itself has acted as a dynamic and demosprudential role-literate participant and focal-point for popular dissent, in particular as a pivotal agency in the operation of accountability networks (Pegram 2008, 2013; Peruzzotti 2012). Such networks operate in a more fluid, flexible and porous way than anything more structured or systematic (Harlow and Rawlings 2007).

In the exercise of this network function the ombud can best be viewed as an appointed 'horizontal accountability mechanism' (O'Donnell 2007) and an instrument of 'oversight' as part of the 'evaluation' function of the 'counter-democratic' movement that seeks to hold to account the executive (Rosanvallon 2008).

Illustration from Argentina and Greece can help demonstrate the point, especially since both Argentina and Greece are re-emergent democracies whose recent past has included military dictatorship, financial crisis and serious challenge to representative democratic practice. Their example is especially salutary in that it accentuates both the possibilities of reimagined options for ombuds and administrative justice more generally, especially in the small places of social rights protection, and the challenge of maintaining innovation in the face of the corrosive and competing values of the globalized marketplace.

Argentina: The Defensoria Del Pueblo

The ombud institution, or *la defensoria del pueblo*, was first introduced in Argentina in 1993 as part of the legacy of the post-dictatorship democratic settlement of 1983. The *defensoria* is rooted in civic republicanism and recognised as a source of justice in that republican context that finds its identity outside the legal and judicial system (Constenla 2013, 2014, 2015).

Far from the ombud being seen as a form of dispute resolution complementary to the courts, the emphasis is on the *defensoria* as a supplement to the legislature as an agent of democratic accountability and human rights values.

The *defensoria* exists, quite deliberately, to limit power, and its chief characteristic is one of attentiveness: the *defensoria* is always on the alert, as explicitly indicated by the designation of the office in some neighbouring Brazilian states as *ouvidoria* ('the auditor' or 'listener'). Such attentiveness has typically led to active engagement of the *defensoria* as part of a wide spectrum of accountability mechanisms with a range of social rights entitlements that includes, for example, disability access to rail travel following the privatization of the state railway, entitlement to public healthcare for non-Argentine nationals, the governance of state-run schools, discrimination in public employment and the organisation of transport networks in Buenos Aires. Most notable, perhaps, is the role of the nine municipal *defensorias* in Buenos Aires in protecting public health services during the economic crisis of 2001/02 that convulsed Argentina and mobilised a mass civil-society movement against the central government.

This picture of the *defensoria* at local level is consistent with that elaborated by political scientist Enrique Peruzzotti in respect of the national *defensoria* (Peruzzotti 2012). Drawing upon Guillermo O'Donnell's classification of social accountability mechanisms in two categories, horizontal and vertical (O'Donnell 2007), Peruzzotti identifies the *defensoria* as a classically 'appointed' component of those horizontal mechanisms located within the intra-state system of checks and balances whose goal is to prevent acts of legal or administrative transgression on the part of the state either by exercising 'police patrol' or, alternatively, 'fire alarm' functions. Inserted within a 'broader web of accountability agencies', their success is, according to Peruzzotti, dependent on the 'proper and coordinated functioning of the whole network' (Peruzzotti 2012: 248).

By way of illustration, he cites the example of the *defensoria's* intervention in a critical environmental dispute in Buenos Aires arising from the historic contamination of a river running through a densely populated metropolitan area and known locally as the Matanza-Riachuelo case. The controversy in question occupied public attention for an extended period between 1992 and a related decision of the Supreme Court of Argentina in June 2006. In the meantime, on Peruzzotti's account, the *defensoria*, responding to two complaints by different 'social actors' about the severe pollution and severe flooding affecting residents, had played a crucial 'articulating role' in the organisation of a broad coalition of state officials and various civil society actors. The result was the creation of a working group comprising local associations, several national NGOs, a national university and the separate *Defensoria de la Ciudad de Buenos Aires.*

For Peruzzotti, crucial in this engagement by the *defensoria* was its persuasive and co-operative mandate as a means of resisting the tendency to confrontation. As he puts it, in this instance: 'the *Defensor* has played a crucial role, acting as a broker between horizontal and social actors…For civil society actors, the *Defensor* provides an accessible entry point to the horizontal network of accountability agencies within the state, serving as a bridge between social accountability initiatives and the intra-state network of horizontal agencies' (Peruzzotti 2012: 265).

The *defensoria* can, in other words, be represented as one of a network of institutions contributing to democratic integrity by holding to account the state at both local and national level against human rights (often social rights) norms, in a context where such entitlements have been marginalised, historically, by political dictatorship and are eroded currently by a recently elected government of overtly 'neoliberal' credentials.

Greece: The Synigoros Tou Politi

The Greek Parliamentary Ombud was established in its current form in April 1997 and opened its doors on 1 October 1998. The primary constitutional task or 'mission' of the Ombud is to mediate between the public administration and private individuals, in order to protect the latter's rights, to ensure the former's compliance with the rule of law, and to combat discrimination (Spanou 2013). The accretion of additional responsibilities since 1998 has supplemented that primary role with the functions of 'protecting and promoting' children's rights and the 'promotion of equal treatment by public administration services' (Greek Ombudsman 2005). As 'mediator', in all these roles the Ombud makes recommendations and proposals to the public administration but does not impose sanctions or annul the illegal actions of the public administration.

The Ombud's equality role has entailed the conduct on behalf of individuals of 'wider investigations', the drafting of 'pertinent' reports, active participation in the co-ordination of relevant state authorities, including collaboration with the then newly founded Equal Treatment Committee in the Ministry of Justice and with the Labour Inspectorate, and the raising of awareness of equality issues within public administration and civil society (Greek Ombudsman 2005). It is noteworthy that in reporting on its activities in 2007, the Greek Ombud gave prominence to its work in co-ordinating and 'mobilizing' other institutional equality bodies and civil society 'in the fight against discrimination' (Greek Ombudsman 2007). The importance of this work was especially acute since the number of individual complaints made (80) was very low and acknowledged by the Ombud as not at all representative of actual levels of discrimination in Greece.

Of particular significance were the steps taken by the Ombud in respect of Roma settlements (Greek Ombudsman 2007: 19–28). In the annual reports for 2005 and 2006 the Ombud had noted various problems of 'structural' social exclusion being experienced by Roma people in respect of education, municipal enrolment and infrastructure for public utility services. As the Ombud reported in 2007, in addition to investigating the relevant individual complaints, the office also continued its practice of initiating investigations and inspecting the settlements across the country (Greek Ombudsman 2007). As a result of these wide-ranging inspections the Ombud was able to cite approximately 20 examples of cases in different parts of the country where the Ombud's interventions had identified institutional problems and successfully proposed longer-term remedial action on the part of the relevant public authority. All the cases identified bear witness to the 'national dimensions' of the Roma issue as well as to the 'compelling need' to implement 'multiple targeted programmes of rehabilitation and social support at a local and regional level' (Greek Ombudsman 2007: 27). Recognising the need for effective co-ordination of such measures across the entire country and noting the 'practical inertia' of the relevant inter-ministerial committee on Roma issues, the Ombud proposed the creation of a new public body to undertake planning in respect of the Roma at a national level and to co-ordinate regional efforts targeted at permanent accommodation, education, utility services, health services, employment opportunities and guarantees of relocation options in the event of lawful eviction (Greek Ombudsman 2007).

Alongside the Roma initiative, the Greek Ombud also published its first special report on an equality issue in November 2009 (Greek Ombudsman 2009). The report represented a comprehensive review of the operation of the gender equality law of 2006 and covered both legislative and policy issues as well as legal, procedural and practical problems. The resulting proposals were closely informed by the empirical experience of investigating 230 relevant complaints between May 2008 and April 2009. In keeping with the approach adopted for Roma issues, the Ombud's concluding proposals concerned what were described as the four 'pillars' of harmonisation of domestic law with European community law, information, prevention and remedy (Greek Ombudsman 2009: 11). In particular, the Ombud concluded that emphasis must be placed on 'preventive action' through regular co-operation and exchange of intelligence with all relevant agencies, social partners and enterprises. This engagement of civil society would supplement efforts to raise citizens' awareness of the Ombud and of equality norms, and reinforce the steps taken by the state to encourage and 'institutionally support' the 'extra-judicial intervention' of the Greek Ombud and its co-operation with the Greek Labour Inspectorate, 'as an alternative to court protection' (Greek Ombudsman 2009: 11).

At the end of its first three years as specialist equality body, the Greek Ombud had concluded that the relatively small number of individual complaints reflected both the unwillingness of individuals to be exposed to publicity about sensitive personal matters and, critically, the mistrust of citizens in the existing institutional mechanisms (Greek Ombudsman 2008). By way of remedy, the Ombud emphasised the need to fill the 'communication gap' between the victims of discrimination and the protective institutions (Greek Ombudsman 2008: 30). The proposed solution was the invigoration of civil society groups, especially in the regional parts of the country, to promote the principle of equal treatment. This entailed outreach work aimed at empowering local advocates to make easier the task of embedding knowledge of the law and confidence in its use.

In short, it was necessary 'to fund specific and targeted activities of approach and/or reception as well as to provide social and legal support to the victims of discriminatory treatment' (Greek Ombudsman 2008: 30). To that end, the Ombud had established a pilot 'communication and co-ordination network' with regional civil society organisations working for the specific protection and assistance of the Roma people. As the Deputy Greek Ombud explained in an interview published in February 2011, the success of the Roma pilot communication and co-ordination network, and of a similar network on asylum and immigration, has prompted plans to develop comparable arrangements in respect of each discrimination ground (Karydis 2011).

The UK: The People's Ombud

These illustrations from Argentina and Greece are reinforced by other examples of accountability networks, formed around an ombud institution, including, for example, in the UK (O'Brien 2011), in Canada (Marin 2006), Australia (McMillan 2009), Peru (Pegram 2008) and Bolivia (Pegram 2013). Specialist disability rights authorities, especially in the UK and Canada, also show how demosprudential interventions have empowered social movements and helped write a new chapter in civil rights history (Vanhala 2011; O'Brien 2016). These examples demonstrate not only that the ombud is an important part of an effective accountability network, but that individualistic legalism is ill-suited to the task of framing ombud activity. Instead, legal pragmatism and demosprudence offer a suitable means for the ombud to realise its distinctive technique, with prioritisation of investigation, interpretation, institutional focus and iteration (O'Brien 2018).

Half a century after Danish Ombudsman Stefan Hurwitz's exhortation to UK policymakers to embrace the Scandinavian ombud institution as a safety-valve for democracy and a tribune of the people, the UK Public Administration Select Committee (PASC) produced a report on the UK Parliamentary Ombudsman and Health Service Ombudsman for England called *Time for a People's Ombudsman* (PASC 2014). The immediate context was the loss of trust in NHS regulation following the damning Francis Report on the Mid-Staffordshire NHS Foundation Trust and the quite separate encouragement from the EU ADR Directive and ODR Regulations for ombuds to see themselves increasingly as mass dispute-resolution mechanisms, especially when digital-era governance, the TripAdvisor mentality, and the decline of publicly funded advice challenged established methods of working. A new style of direct popular engagement seemed possible, and indeed necessary, in an era of unparalleled technological empowerment.

PASC responded with a programme of simplification and rationalisation, with proposals for a single portal for all public service complaints, a single Public Service Ombudsman for England, and a single Cabinet Office minister with responsibility for complaints and ombud policy. The title of the PASC report points more fundamentally towards the need for renewed democratic engagement.

In the context of UK ombud reform, there are already elements of PHSO and LGSCO practice that presage a demosprudential future. Some of those elements are acknowledged in the independent evaluation of PHSO published in 2018 and entitled *Value for Money* (Tyndall et al. 2018): the development of outreach work through initiatives such as Radio Ombudsman, through which the ombud produces a podcast of interviews with a range of people, including other practitioners and aggrieved citizens; the increased transparency of outcomes and of communication more generally, including in the case of the LGSCO the online publication of every decision made by the ombud; the purposeful publication of special thematic reports on issues such as mental health, sepsis and the treatment of eating disorders, and in the case of the LGSCO on special educational needs or refuse collection; the re-articulated aspiration to acquire own-initiative investigation powers, complaints design-authority powers, and scope to develop flexible methods of response to grievance.

In the recent PHSO past as well there is precedent for a demosprudential approach that has, for example, combined NGO activism with the invocation of human rights principle on behalf of disabled citizens who had died whilst in NHS secondary care (O'Brien 2011). Indeed, examples of similar approaches can be traced back even further, for example to the Channel Tunnel investigation during the early 1990s, which arose from several complaints raised by different MPs on behalf of their constituents and which were treated as representative of more widespread concerns throughout southeast England (Harlow and Rawlings 2007).

All public sector ombuds are part of a network of accountability, a web of institutions with distinct, and sometimes overlapping, responsibilities for oversight of public administration. They operate within these networks to varying degrees of engagement—treading what can be a thin line between their own work and that of regulators and auditors is itself a design challenge, particularly in areas crowded with regulators, such as health and social care. Yet failing to assert their distinct role risks removing the democratic voice that comes through, and sometimes only through, the work of the ombuds. The key is 'co-operation', or the 'craft' of working together. Manzini cites Sennett and his definition of co-operation 'as an exchange in which the participants benefit from the encounter' (Manzini 2015: 93). Co-operation need not be tied to closeness or to consensus (Sennett 2018: 259); instead it is 'sociality', a kind of bond with others 'based on sharing an impersonal task', based on 'doing something together rather than being together' (Sennett 2018: 260). Collaboration is about encounter and exchange to achieve a shared benefit or value. It also requires adopting and abiding by some shared rules and building both strong and weak social ties (Manzini 2015: 101). Weak ties have value in that they make the collaboration more open and accessible; strong ties give stability and make for a 'healthy social fabric' (Manzini 2015: 102).

The value of fostering both weak and strong ties echoes the aims of mediation—to give weight to different perspectives and voices equally, to prioritise collaboration rather than competition, to step away from the need to 'prove' one's case, and to agree jointly on actions—which may or may not be 'resolutions'. Mediation can be used as a mechanism for co-equal citizens' voices to be heard and to shape jointly and 'frame' the issues in dispute. This could be followed by an appropriate mechanism—fact-finding investigation if necessary, or order to act, or remedial actions. It allows for non-closure, or partial closure, with agreed next steps as a crucial outcome. Mediation as a technique works with the ombud technique of investigation on several levels—including engaging all interested parties in shaping the issues, giving space for understanding varied perspectives, highlighting what facts require investigation, exploring needs that will address the issue of remedy where fault is found.

Compassion and an Ethic of Care: The Judge Who Cried

It has become increasingly apparent that even demosprudential approaches that accommodate network governance, democratic experimentalism and problem-solving courts lack an essential ingredient if they are truly to serve the public good. In the US context, the presidency of Barack Obama, and in particular the high hopes it entertained for substantive reform in healthcare, labour law, immigration and education, has been perceived as a watershed. From the disappointment of such promise has emerged a new form of social realism that takes more generous account than even network governance, democratic experimentalism or problem-solving courts of human emotion in 'process architecture'. It has, for example, been persuasively argued that the deliberatively democratic and consensus-building 'town hall' meetings that were intended to show how mediation-like processes could be used to encourage deliberative consideration of healthcare proposals in fact quickly descended into adversarial encounters, in which passions ran high and broke the boundaries of public reasoning that had been expected to enable a more collaborative exercise of power (Menkel-Meadow 2011). It has even been suggested that such experience reinforces the argument that dispute-system design is incapable of escaping the

Anglo-American indulgence of adversarialism so that it becomes a 'universal procedure of fairness and good decision-making' (Menkel-Meadow 2011: 5; Hampshire 2000).

As a result, the need to take account of emotion and the affective aspects of responding to grievance is all the more urgent. What is needed is deliberative discourse that adopts a 'passions' mode and allows for scaling up so that it can provide innovative structures for social conversation in the context of responding to citizen grievance (Menkel-Meadow 2011; Nussbaum 2013, 2018). The challenge becomes that of reimagining the design required to allow all sides to be heard properly when there are profound differences, not just of belief and value but of feeling. It is only when we have given due allowance to the way in which what we feel affects what we think, reason and believe that the complexity of the challenge becomes clear and the need to avoid polarised and binary process-design compelling (Menkel-Meadow 2011).

In a jurisprudential context, the most promising way of giving recognition to the emotional aspects of response to grievance is by invoking the concept of compassion as the core of an ethic of care. Whilst the 'ethic of care' literature might not give much encouragement to the idea that formal justice should be used to enforce norms of compassion, it does offer support for the view that informal justice processes should seek to foster compassionate relational care, so that relational rights are substantive, and compassion or care a central component of procedure (Herring 2013a, b, 2017). It has been suggested, for example, that legalism is based on the assumption that the individual is competent, independent and detached. The priority then becomes the protection of rights to self-determination and autonomy, with strong boundaries to ward off interference from others. The reality is, however, that we are vulnerable and interdependent, and that our strength lies not in our autonomy but in our relationship with others (Herring 2017; Nussbaum 2004). The starting point in that case becomes 'a norm of interlocking mutually dependent relationships, rather than an individualised vision of rights. Rights and interests are not designed to protect individuals per se, so much as upholding and maintaining networks of caring relationships' (Herring 2017: 162).

There is a view that norms should not, and cannot, take account of compassionate caring relationships because any such norms are necessarily universal and abstract rules to be invoked after concrete relationships have already broken down. Against this it has been argued that the purpose of such norms is, on the contrary, to exert influence outside formal dispute resolution processes, such as courts. It is on this account more important, for example, to create an environment in which compassionate caring relationships can flourish than to bring careless healthcare staff to court to be chastised and 'fined'. Similarly, whereas traditional notions of negative rights attach entitlement to individuals and promote libertarian values, a more relational approach, whilst acknowledging the individual as a separate 'person', would nevertheless place such a person within 'a web of relationships of care, attachments and interdependency' (Herring 2017: 165). Far from celebrating and enforcing abstract rules, the response to grievance would instead prioritise the virtue of attentiveness to affliction, starting with the context and concrete reality of particular situations and relationships.

In the light of these insights from the 'ethic of care' literature, we can get beyond the notion of 'judging as nudging' and so to a broader vision of informal justice that takes account of emotion. Instead of decision-making or response to grievance being seen as entailing an exclusive form of rationality and cognitive detachment, a more responsive approach takes account of the parties' beliefs and values and feelings, and therefore enables a more meaningful and conversational style of engagement in a language that reflects the concrete and affective reality of the situation rather than cognitive abstraction from it. To that extent, the process for responding to grievance both encourages and expresses care and compassion. As Jonathan Herring has observed, in the context of arguing that the law can promote care and compassion by sending messages that influence attitudes, make emotional sense and interpret rights in a more relational way: 'The law at its most basic level is dealing with and responding to people. People are governed by their emotions, and caring relationships play a key part in their lives. This will require a major restructuring of the law and society. The primary aim will not then be economic productivity, but the promotion and protection of caring compassionate relationships' (Herring 2017: 169). And we might add, the 'judge who cried' might in time become a more familiar spectacle (Sachs 2009).

The Demosprudential Ombud: Community, Network, Openness and a 'Duty of Active Kindness'

These examples of the ombud, both in the UK and elsewhere, and of the courts when grappling with social rights concerns, disclose an incipient form of demosprudential practice in shaping a response to public grievance. Such developments implicitly reinforce the values of community, network and openness as a framework for democratic credibility and for equality. They build also on the inherent tendency of the ombud institution towards practices that privilege investigation, interpretation, iteration and institutional focus. How might such implicit reinforcement be made explicit, and what would be the anticipated consequences for the key relationships between the ombud, citizen and state?

The first element of ombud technique to consider is investigation. Some argue that investigation is old-fashioned and cumbersome, too labour-intensive and ponderous for agile modern expectations (Tyndall et al. 2018). The version of demosprudential investigation proposed here is not that. It is instead a vehicle for engaging not just individual aggrieved citizens and public authorities but broader community perspectives. If the ombud is to achieve that she must be accessible, which means there is no place for devices like legislative filters or prescribed forms of complaint, such as 'in writing'. More than that, expression of grievance will not be subject to a victim test but, as in Indian public interest litigation, there will be scope for the ombud to receive intelligence from any source and exercise discretion on how to respond. An example is the first own-initiative investigation to be carried out by the Northern Ireland Public Services Ombudsman (NIPSO), into the way the Department for Communities administers Personal Independence Payments (PIPs, formerly Disability Living Allowance). In addition to having received 'a significant number of complaints' about PIPs, NIPSO took account of the high number of appeals of the Department's internal review decisions that are overturned at tribunal and its own assessment of the Department's procedures, concluding that enough evidence existed to prompt a systemic investigation (NIPSO Press release, 21 January 2019).

Such freedom of process will enable the ombud to hear and see more acutely; more importantly, it will enable the community to have a voice, and more particularly to give expression to those whose actual voices are rarely heard. Investigation of this sort will enable the ombud to act as a focal point for the expression of collective dissent and to respond as a role-literate participant who is a central source of catalysing energy in the co-ordination of a broader accountability network, comprising other agencies. In that way, the ombud is indeed an outlet not just for an old democracy but for civil society as an active expression of complex and layered social space, set free from the rigid polarities of individual and state. In the to-and-fro of ombud investigation, the prioritisation of relationships with informed civil society groups, NGOs, charities, advice agencies will add to individual grievance a communitarian perspective, a network of overlapping interest, and a measure of openness to innovation that transcends the individualism, systematisation and closure of a legalistic mentality. The explicit adoption of such practices is the way forward for the demosprudential ombud both in its egalitarian aspirations and in its deference to public value and the common good.

The second element is interpretation. Demosprudential interpretation entails the availability of a language that is both democratic and emancipatory and that captures the fully human dimension of citizen grievance. It is easy to reduce the death of a learning-disabled person in NHS care into the anodyne language of maladministration or poor service. To preserve the force and human dimension of such a complaint, a richer conceptual framework is needed, not of rules but of principles. Such a resource already exists in the language of human rights, especially social rights, not as an easy panacea but as a tool for interpreting grievance in its stark reality and in terms that make sense to those who have taken the trouble to give voice to otherwise latent dissent. The prioritisation of human rights language is not a route to the legalistic application of rules or the pretence of adjudication on civil rights disputes. It is instead recognition that human rights offer privileged access to a set of interlocking democratic values that have social, as well as political, bite. Once reinserted in their original social-democratic context, the inseparability of social and civil rights yields values of fairness, respect, equality, dignity and autonomy that can frame other more specific or sectoral guides to virtuous behaviour. The ombud can then take its place as part of a much broader network not just of regulatory agencies but of human rights institutions working in a complementary way to shape relationships between citizen and state that are humane and marked by a duty of active kindness.

The third element is iteration. The demosprudential ombud will adopt an approach that is responsive to different perspectives and that privileges the deliberative interplay of those perspectives in the achievement of the public good. To that extent, the iterative practices of the ombud, in exchanging views and eliciting evidence, in sharing perspectives and provisional assessments, will amount to a form of public reasoning that is communitarian and open, and itself expressive of the human rights principles of fairness, equality, dignity, respect and autonomy. The ombud will in effect fulfil the role of facilitator in the construction of a deliberative exchange conducted within the framework of broad human rights principle, keeping open the possibility of dialogue with the careful avoidance of premature closure.

The fourth element is institutional focus. The demosprudential ombud, whilst open to the investigation of individual grievance, is mindful to prioritise the public good and so realise genuine public value in the outcomes she achieves. The emphasis will to that extent be upon future prevention rather than remedial cure, and upon the restoration of constructive relationship. The ability to provide remedy will therefore prioritise not so much financial or other redress (valuable and indeed necessary though these may also be for the individual) but systemic and institutional change. The restoration achieved in this way will be a matter for long-term community oversight and evaluation, not just short-term individual satisfaction. The process of humanising the bureaucracy is communitarian, networked and open, and rarely immediate in its achievement or susceptible to objective metric.

Finally, it was noted earlier that in the 1960s the extra-legal aspiration for the then new ombud institution was that it should inaugurate a 'cult of bureaucratic humanity' and an 'active duty of kindness'. More recently (Zacka 2017) it has been emphasised once again that the aim of administrative justice should not be limited to the hygienic surveillance of good decision-making but should instead extend to the promotion of virtuous behaviour among street-level bureaucrats, to the cultivation of virtuous disposition and so to the support of an environment in which such dispositions might flourish. The focus is as a result cultural, pertaining to affective aspects as well as cognitive, not merely administrative.

* * *

By attending to aggrieved individuals as part of a web of communitarian relationships, by adopting human rights, especially social rights, norms, by participating with other agencies in networks of deliberative decision-making and mutually reinforcing support, and by seeking restorative legacies of her interventions, the ombud will implicitly model an ethic of care and promote compassion as an overriding disposition. Beyond that and the general attentiveness to affliction that demosprudential practice entails, the demosprudential ombud will not fight shy of using language that is explicitly ethical rather than legal, capable of capturing the full dimension of grievance and of the environmental change that may prove necessary to effect sustainable and innovative restoration of constructive relationship. If judges can cry, and sometimes laugh, then so can ombuds.

References

Berman, G., & Feinblatt, J. (2001). *Problem-Solving Courts: A Brief Primer.* New York: Center for Court Innovation.

Chayes, A. (1976). The Role of the Judge in Public Law Litigation. *Harvard Law Review, 89*, 1281–1316.

Constenla, C. (2013). Del Monte Sacro a Salvador de Bahia: Sobre quien podria ser el Defensor del Pueblo. *Revista de la Asociacion de Derecho Administrativo de la Ciudad Autonoma de Buenos Aires, 5*, 195–208.

Constenla, C. (2014). Defensor del Pueblo: un enemigo del pueblo? *Eforos, Publicacion Semestral del Instituto Latinoamericano del Ombudsman-Defensor del Pueblo*, June–December, 21–30.

Constenla, C. (2015). El Defensor del Pueblo in Latin America. *Visioni Latino-Americane, 12*, 59–72.

Dorf, M., & Sabel, C. (1998). A Constitution of Democratic Experimentalism. *Columbia Law Review, 98*, 267–473.

Fredman, S. (2008). *Human Rights Transformed: Positive Rights and Positive Duties.* Oxford: OUP.

Greek Ombudsman. (2005). *Annual Report.* Athens: Greek Ombudsman.

Greek Ombudsman. (2007). *Annual Report.* Athens: Greek Ombudsman.

Greek Ombudsman. (2008). *Promoting Equal Treatment: The Greek Ombudsman as National Equality Body.* Athens: Greek Ombudsman.

Greek Ombudsman. (2009). *Equal Treatment of Men and Women in Employment and Labour Relations.* Athens: Greek Ombudsman.

Guinier, L. (2013). Courting the People: Demosprudence and the Law/Politics Divide. *Harvard Law Review, 127*(423), 437–444.

Guinier, L., & Torres, G. (2014). Changing the Wind: Notes towards a Demosprudence of Law and Social Movements. *Yale Law Journal, 123*, 2742–2804.

Gutmann, A., & Thompson, D. (2004). *Why Deliberative Democracy?* Princeton: Princeton University Press.

Hampshire, S. (2000). *Justice is Conflict.* Princeton, NJ: Princeton University Press.

Harlow, C., & Rawlings, R. (2007). Promoting Accountability in Multilevel Governance: A Network Approach. *European Law Journal, 13*, 542–562.

Herring, J. (2013a). Forging a Relational Approach: Best Interests or Human Rights? *Medical Law International, 13*(1), 32–54.

Herring, J. (2013b). *Caring and the Law.* Oxford: Hart.

Herring, J. (2017). Compassion, Ethics of Care and Legal Rights. *International Journal of Law in Context, 13*(2), 158–171.

Hertogh, M. (2001). Coercion, Co-operation and Control: Understanding the Policy Impact of Administrative Courts and the Ombudsman in the Netherlands. *Law and Policy, 23*, 47–67.

Karydis, V. (2011). *The Greek Equality Body in the Spotlight*. Brussels: Equinet.

Khilnani, S., Raghavan, V., & Thiruvengadam, A. (2012). Revisiting the Role of the Judiciary in Plural Societies. In S. Khilnani, V. Raghavan, & A. Thiruvengadam (Eds.), *Comparative Constitutionalism in South Asia*. New Delhi: OUP.

Klein, A. (2007). Judging as Nudging: New Governance Approaches for the Enforcement of Constitutional Social and Economic Rights. *Columbia Human Rights Law Review, 39*, 351–422.

Manzini, E. (2015). *Design, When Everybody Designs: An Introduction to Design for Social Innovation*. Cambridge, MA: MIT Press.

Marin, A. (2006). Innovate or Perish. *Canadian Journal of Administrative Law and Practice, 20*, 101–115.

McMillan, J. (2009). *The Ombudsman's Role in Human Rights Protection—An Australian Perspective*. Paper to the Eleventh Asian Ombudsman Association Conference, Bangkok, 2–5 November 2009.

Menkel-Meadow, C (2004/2005). The Lawyer's Role(s) in Deliberative Democracy. *Nevada Law Journal, 5*, 347–369.

Menkel-Meadow, C. (2006, Winter). Deliberative Democracy and Conflict Resolution: Two Theories and Practices of Participation in the Polity. *Dispute Resolution Magazine*, pp. 18–22.

Menkel-Meadow, C. (2011). Scaling Up Deliberative Democracy as Dispute Resolution in Healthcare Reform: A Work in Progress. *Law and Contemporary Problems, 74*(1), 1–30.

Nussbaum, M. (2004). *Hiding from Humanity: Disgust, Shame, and the Law*. Princeton: Princeton University Press.

Nussbaum, M. (2013). *Political Emotions: Why Love Matters for Justice*. Cambridge, MA: Harvard University Press.

Nussbaum, M. (2018). *The Monarchy of Fear: A Philosopher Looks at our Political Crisis*. Oxford: OUP.

O'Brien, N. (2011). Law and "The Good Life": Learning Disability, Equality and Healthcare in the UK. *The Equal Rights Review, 6*, 83–96.

O'Brien, N. (2016). Disability Discrimination Law in the United Kingdom and the New Civil Rights History: The Contribution of Caroline Gooding. *Journal of Law and Society, 43*(3), 444–468.

O'Brien, N. (2018). Ombudsmen and Public Authorities: A Modest Proposal. In M. Hertogh & R. Kirkham (Eds.), *Research Handbook on The Ombudsman*. Cheltenham: Edward Elgar.

O'Donnell, G. (2007). *Dissonances: Democratic Critiques of Democracy*. Notre Dame, IN: University of Notre Dame.

Pegram, T. (2008). Accountability in Hostile Times: The Case of the Peruvian Human Rights Ombudsman 1996–2001. *Journal of Latin American Studies, 40*, 51–82.
Pegram, T. (2013). The Bolivian Human Rights Ombudsman and Economic, Social and Cultural Rights. In E. Brems, G. de Beco, & W. Vandenhole (Eds.), *National Human Rights Institutions, and Economic, Social and Cultural Rights*. Antwerp: Intersentia.
Peruzzotti, E. (2012). The Societalization of Horizontal Accountability: Rights Advocacy and the Defensor del Pueblo de la Nacion in Argentina. In R. Goodman & T. Pegram (Eds.), *Human Rights, State Compliance, and Social Change*. Cambridge: CUP.
Public Administration Select Committee (PASC). (2014). Time for a People's Ombudsman. *Fourteenth Report of Session 2013–14*. London: House of Commons.
Ray, B. (2011). Demosprudence in Comparative Perspective. *Stanford Journal of International Law, 47*, 111–173.
Rosanvallon, P. (2008). *Counter-Democracy: Politics in an Age of Distrust*. Cambridge: CUP.
Sabel, C., & Simon, W. (2004). Destabilization Rights: How Public Law Litigation Succeeds. *Harvard Law Review, 117*, 1016–1101.
Sachs, A. (2009). *The Strange Alchemy of Life and Law*. Oxford: OUP.
Sennett, R. (2018). *Building and Dwelling*. London: Allen Lane.
Simon, W. (2004). Solving Problems v Claiming Rights: The Pragmatist Challenge to Legal Liberalism. *William and Mary Law Review, 46*, 127–212.
Simon, W. (2009). The Warren Court, Legalism and Democracy: Sketch for a Critique in a Style Learned from Morton Horwitz. *Columbia Law School, Public Law and Legal Theory Working Group Paper No. 09-196.*
Spanou, C. (2013). *The Greek Ombudsman and Public Administration during Challenging Times*. 13th Annual Lecture of the Hellenic Observatory, European Institute, London School of Economics, 25 November 2013. Retrieved from www.macropolis.gr.
Tyndall, P., Mitchell, C., & Gill, C. (2018). *Value for Money*. London: PHSO.
Vanhala, L. (2011). *Making Rights a Reality? Disability Rights Activists and Legal Mobilization*. Cambridge: CUP.
Zacka, B. (2017). *When the State Meets the Street: Public Service and Moral Agency*. Cambridge, MA: Harvard University Press.

CHAPTER 7

Administrative Justice: A Demosprudential Fabric

Abstract This chapter expands the focus from the ombud to the wider administrative justice fabric and considers how the values of community, network and openness can contribute to a form of demosprudence that helps realise relational human rights in the small places of daily life. The importance of looking, listening and even 'touching' in that endeavour is acknowledged. The chapter reflects on the demosprudential implications for the practice of mediation, of tribunals and of public inquiries. It takes special educational needs as a case study in which the potential for interwoven networks between different administrative justice institutions is especially apparent. The chapter also considers the opportunities and challenges posed by technological innovation, digital design and the emergence of 'super-complaints'.

Keywords Mediation • Tribunals • Public inquiries • Super-complaints • Digitalisation • Participation • Recognition

A Fabric of Interwoven Relationships

The ombud has been presented as the model of a demosprudential institution whose use of the techniques of investigation, iteration, interpretation and institutional focus allows it to be a force for 'bringing social rights home' and to put into practice the concepts of community, network and openness. Its ability to focus on dialogic, participative processes, and its

M. Doyle, N. O'Brien, *Reimagining Administrative Justice*,
https://doi.org/10.1007/978-3-030-21388-6_7

prioritising of influence over formal enforcement powers, make the ombud uniquely placed to identify social rights as being at the heart of administrative justice principles and of the everyday interactions between citizen and state. How might other parts of the fabric of administrative justice do the same, adopting techniques appropriate to their distinctive role to enhance democratic participation? And how might these different parts, different actors, weave together in a way that fosters recognition and acknowledgement not only of individual grievance and the collective interest but of these parts' distinct but interdependent relationships?

An earlier chapter set out how Law's Empire has dominated administrative justice, so that in the relationship between ombuds and courts, for example, it is clear who is the junior partner. A similar subjugation has occurred with other 'mechanisms' of administrative justice—tribunals, mediation and public inquiries have, at different stages and in different ways, been set on a course that would further enmesh them in the web of legalism. The problems this creates are many and varied, not least the erosion of trust in the institutions of the state and of administrative justice. As political theorist Danielle Allen has noted, 'citizenship is not, fundamentally, a matter of institutional duties but of how one learns to negotiate loss and reciprocity. … unrestrained self-interest does not make the world go round but corrodes the bases of trust' (Allen 2004: 165).

This chapter explores the practices of demosprudential mediators, tribunals, and inquiries and their potential place as part of a networked and loosely woven administrative justice fabric.

The use of the senses is relevant here, as it is in the work of the ombud—looking, listening, even touching, where that suggests a lingering feeling of empathy, of common humanity inherent in the ethic of care approach that starts with 'a norm of interlocking, mutually dependent relationships' (Herring 2017: 162). Ombuds, tribunals and mediators being described as 'extra-judicial' mechanisms suggests that they are 'less than' the courts, their powers limited to making recommendations rather than issuing legally binding precedents. In fact, in contrast with the courts, whose aim is to prohibit bad behaviour—to 'stop us being little devils, not making us little angels' (Herring 2017: 161)—so-called extra-judicial institutions of administrative justice are about promoting good behaviour on behalf of the community, including good administration. They are therefore well suited to restoring the humanity in bureaucracy, to ensuring that the way we touch the state, and it touches us, is constructive, not destructive. The 'often small, but very tangible, transactions between the individual and the State' are like door handles, with 'tactile qualities' that are vital to shaping both perceptions and relationships (Design Council 2004: 40–43)—an unexpected analogy but one that captures the role of administrative justice institutions in fostering community over individualism, network over system, and openness over closure.

Mediation as 'Appropriate Alternative' or 'Collaborative Complement'?

Mediation as an independent mechanism operates within administrative justice in specific but shadowy corners—shadowy because little is published about its use, and the traditional requirement that mediation is confidential acts as a shroud of secrecy so that even those involved feel constrained from discussing it. The confidentiality requirement so ingrained in the model of mediation used for individual civil claims, however, does not have the same primacy in mediation in cases involving public interest. An example is the commitment of the Home Office not to insist on confidentiality agreements when settling (by mediation or otherwise) redress claims from victims of the Windrush generation scandal (NAO 2018, para 18). Two areas in particular illustrate the need for a model that embraces democratic participation and the relaxing of confidentiality rules: planning and development, and special educational needs and disabilities. In both contexts, at least one of the parties is a public authority with requirements to report (to auditors, for example) or to answer to democratically elected representatives (local authority councillors, for example), and both involve consideration of wider community interests (CEDR 2003). Therefore, it may be both undesirable and unfeasible to impose confidentiality on mediation of public sector cases, including but not only multi-party public policy disputes.

In planning, the use of mediation has been advocated for some years as a means of hearing the interests of, for example, third parties who have no effective voice in the planning appeals process, and of facilitating views on development and its impact on the wider communities in which it takes place. It is an area of 'deep-value differences' encompassing public and private interests and wider community norms, in use for decades by, for example, the Land and Environment Court in New South Wales, Australia (Pearce and Stubbs 2000: 1338). Mediation does not replace statutory decision-making on planning but offers a complementary process that 'may assist in improving the quality of an application, or may serve to resolve or narrow a dispute', thereby potentially helping the planning process 'to arrive at better informed and more cost-effective outcomes' (Scottish Government 2009: 1). An example is the restructuring of the municipalities of Cape Town in South Africa following the end of apartheid (as set out in Scottish Government 2009: 16). The strategic challenge faced by the city was to restructure to allow for racial integration in a previously segregated population. Using mediation involving three key groups—mediators, planners and stakeholders referred to as 'champions', representing a broad range of interests—the process entailed restructuring what had been 47 municipalities into 7 new ones. Used in conjunction with consensus-building and community engagement, mediation forms part of wider consultation, decision-making and investigation processes that recognise a number of interests, both collective and individual.

Critiques of claims for mediation's advantages of speed, low-cost, and informality are justifiable (Pearce and Stubbs 2000; Bondy et al. 2005), but in a public interest context it is the promised multi-interest engagement that is more interesting to explore—its added value more than its alleged proportionality. Even this, especially in the context of planning, is subject to criticism, however, and particularly to criticism that the interests of local councillors and national government are insufficiently represented. The lack of 'supervision' of mediation contrasts with that in formal planning appeals, where the adjudicator's role is 'to ensure that all significant third-party or public interests (including those of central government) are taken into account and that there is openness and accountability' (Pearce and Stubbs 2000: 1346). Evidence that mediation used in planning disputes delivers on these promises is, so far, not conclusive; it is a case more of potential than realisation, but that potential is worth exploring. Mediation and consensus-building approaches have been used in a number of 'experiments' of community-wide disputes, described by Menkel-Meadow as experiments that draw on participatory democracy and democratic discourse in terms of political theory, and on mediation theory and practice in terms of process (Menkel-Meadow 2002: 51). With the right institutional support, inclusive design and appropriate mediation techniques, such interests—and those interests less likely to be asserted, such as those of minority groups without representation—would be given equal voice.

Special Educational Needs: A Case Study

Where mediation has gained more traction, particularly in recent years, is in special educational needs and disabilities (SEND) disputes in England and Additional Support Needs in Scotland. In England, the Children and Families Act 2014 gave mediation a more prominent role as a complement to, on the one hand, informal engagement between parents and local authorities, and on the other, the formal adjudication of the First-Tier Tribunal (SEND). Embedded in the English SEND statutory Code of Practice since 2001 as a means of resolving disagreements between parents, schools and local authorities, mediation's role was expanded in 2014 to cover from birth to age 25 and to include early years settings and colleges as well as health and social care needs. This wider remit brings in a wider range of agencies and providers (Clinical Commissioning Groups, social workers, colleges and apprenticeship-providers) who must work together to implement the policy goals of the legislation—goals that encompass inclusion, participation and accountability. That health and social care are to be considered holistically alongside education opens the way toward a more networked response to grievance. For appeals against local authority decisions that involve these other issues as well as education, the Tribunal is operating a national trial that gives it the power to make recommendations to health and social care providers alongside its binding decisions on local authority SEND departments. The design of this trial reflects the principle of networked openness underlying a reimagined administrative justice.

So too does the wider network of actors involved in the disputes and complaints landscape related to SEND in England. In 2017, nearly 2500 SEND mediations were conducted; in 2016–17, 1599 SEND tribunal hearings were held (Department for Education 2018; Ministry of Justice 2017). The Local Government and Social Care Ombudsman (LGSCO) has seen an increase in the number of complaints about how local authorities have dealt with SEND issues and has published a number of Focus Reports related to SEND (LGSCO 2017; LGO 2014). This is a complex and multi-faceted landscape, with a range of complaint mechanisms for different types of disputes operated by different public bodies and private actors (schools, local authorities, Secretary of State, the NHS, Ofsted, the SEND Tribunal, mediation, ombud, judicial review). It is, like planning, an area in which the polycentricity of disputes and the tension between individual rights and collective public interest are at play.

Despite its traditional conception as one of several forms of alternative or appropriate dispute resolution, in the SEND context mediation is not a matter of settlement and in that sense does not prioritise closure. The impetus for mediation may be to consider how the parties in dispute can agree on a specific issue, or issues, that otherwise would be decided by the Tribunal, but in reality the mediation encompasses a multiplicity of issues that go beyond the grounds for appeal, reflecting the ongoing relationship between families and the schools and local government departments responsible for educating children. It is not only the interests and needs—including the need to be heard and acknowledged, to communicate—of the parties attending that have to be taken into account. Collective interests are inherent in the duties that local authority SEND teams have for accounting for use of public funds, in schools' needs to be supported, and in the needs of all pupils in the community to have access to appropriate education. As a means of co-design, along the lines that Manzini suggests, mediation offers the promise of addressing both individual and collective needs; it is essentially about connection, and it embraces conflict as a positive force for change. In that way, it allows for many voices and lends itself to the polycentric nature of SEND disputes.

The 'Sensibility' of Mediation

The ability of mediation to accommodate many voices and issues gives it a distinct texture or 'sensibility' that can complement more determinative grievance mechanisms. Mediation works in tandem with tribunals, as in the SEND context, and with the ombud; disputes can be mediated before or even after an ombud investigation, for example (LGSCO 2017: 7; OIA 2013). It can also function as a complement to judicial review and the Court of Protection, often in complex cases in which disability rights are at the core (Bondy and Doyle 2011; May 2017). More often, however, mediation has been presented as an alternative, not a complement, to more formal legal processes and even as an answer to the problems besetting the courts, 'gridlocked with competing sides or overworked with too-big-to-handle dockets' (Menkel-Meadow 2002: 53–54). A similar sense of gridlock has arisen in the past in relation to the built environment, and in the same way that 'planning' attempts to solve a perceived problem (overcrowding) that may or may not reflect reality (Mae Architects 2014), in the justice 'system' a similar sense of overcrowding gives rise to the need to manage (decrease) demand for a limited resource—in this case expensive court and tribunal time and the expense of judicial decision-making. The emphasis on mediation, from Lord Woolf's *Access to Justice* report in 1996 through to proportionate dispute resolution as advocated in the 2004 White Paper, the 2007 Act, and the 2016 *Transforming Our Justice System* paper, set out to promote informal mechanisms of resolution as an answer to the perceived 'problem' of overcrowding in the formal justice system. Taking a cue from Mae Architects' suggestion to get rid of planning, it may be that to some extent, non-design, a hands-off approach, is needed to accommodate the looseness that enables mediation to be more than about resolution or settlement. For Mae Architects, this involves a *plan* versus *planning*, and its principles are compatible with fostering democratic engagement and accountability, mutualism and difference, rather than the conventional principles on which cities are founded of 'centre, enclosure and boundaries' (Mae Architects 2014: 135). Such a shift does not prioritise cost and speed as the imperatives.

These principles of 'plan' versus 'planning' resonate with what has been called the transformative dimension of mediation, linked to 'an emerging new vision of self and society, one based on relational connection and understanding rather than on individual autonomy alone' (Bush and Folger 2005: 23–24). This reflects a shift from an individualistic vision to a relational and interactive one, bringing individual freedoms together with social conscience—with mediation, and its prioritising of recognition over resolution, as one of the key processes through which to express this new vision. In contrast with Sennett's 'sociality', settlement-oriented behaviour by mediators (often encouraged not only by policy imperatives but by codes of conduct and practice standards) is linked to wider issues of 'social separation' and 'conflict control', akin to the control Sennett describes as being exercised by closed networks (Sennett 2018). Bush and Folger identify an underlying ideology that is fundamentally pessimistic and that holds that because human beings are 'incapable of engaging with one another without destructive consequences', social interaction is a destructive force (Bush and Folger 2005: 247). If this seems over-dramatic, consider the language used in some descriptions of the mediator's role—to 'control' the process, 'manage' emotions, helping people to move away from 'unreasonable' positions—and some techniques, including keeping parties apart in caucus sessions, coercion and even bullying by mediators (Genn et al. 2007; Enterkin and Sefton 2006). Mediation is not about neutrality, contrary to popular belief, nor is it about managing or controlling conflict. Concerns about the dangers of interaction are rooted in the view that individuals are driven by desire of fulfilment and that interaction must be limited and controlled so it meets that need but does not spill over into conflict, which is something to be managed in what is called 'conflict control'. A 'conflict-control' model relies on a deficit view of human capacity linked to an 'ideology of individualism' and a notion that social interaction should be 'tolerated but watched carefully' (Bush and Folger 2005: 245).

There is a similar boundary-setting in the approach by caseworkers in ombuds. Consider the emphasis placed on 'expectations management' as a way to minimise conflict (Gilad 2008). The need to resist 'conflict control' echoes much of what Allen says about how to build trust among strangers through the fostering of 'political friendship'. The emphasis on 'early resolution' by ombuds (Doyle et al. 2014) betrays the impoverished nature of the ombud endeavour when measured against New Public Management efficiency targets of 'cost per case' and backlog reduction. In transporting the quick-win potential of mediation into an ombuds context, much of this transformational potential is lost. Rather than measuring the success of mediation by the number of settlements achieved—an acceptable ambition, perhaps, in the context of civil and commercial disputes—we should be aiming for mediation to be measured in terms of sustainability—whether it offers an alternative to the assembly line of complaints and appeals that the administrative justice 'system' increasingly appears to be. When the interaction between people in conflict is open, not focused on settlement, when it is 'humanised', whatever comes out (which might or might not be some form of resolution) 'will have a different meaning and quality than it would otherwise have' (Bush and Folger 2005: 250).

Menkel-Meadow suggests that just as architects, planners and lay users come together as 'spatial agents' in designing the public realm, so too mediators are reshaping the processes they use to move away from a focus on resolution and 'right answers' to focus on the 'sensibility' of mediation, one that adopts a feminist emphasis on needs and that prioritises empathy and listening rather than closure (Menkel-Meadow 2016). She writes of what she considers to be 'mediation values'—reconciliation, listening, storytelling, empathy, understanding, accountability and apology, if not forgiveness—being used in a restorative way in both large and small arenas, including in human rights claims and in controversial community-wide issues. Just as Allen describes a decision taken as the start, not end, of the democratic process (Allen 2004: 117), Menkel-Meadow, citing divisive

US Supreme Court judgements of *Roe v Wade* and *Brown v Board of Education*, argues that implementation of these judgements would have been improved had some form of facilitated deliberative dialogue been put in place (Menkel-Meadow 2002: 40–41). In this way, she argues against Lon Fuller's position that each dispute process has its own morality and should be kept separate; a keen advocate of 'process pluralism', Menkel-Meadow thinks we need now to consider mixing up these processes to achieve more sustainable outcomes.

Tribunals: Beyond a 'Court Substitute' Function

The Franks Report in 1957 stated that tribunals were not part of the 'machinery of administration' but a means of 'adjudication', which, as Drewry makes clear, led Franks 'down the road of increased legal formality and judicialisation' (Drewry 2009). That process of judicialisation found expression, for example, in the appointment of legally qualified chairs, legal representation, 'orderly procedures' of a quasi-judicial kind, hearings routinely in public, decisions reasoned in quasi-judicial form and the right of appeal to a court in accordance with tightly defined conditions. Franks was the first attempt at system design of administrative justice, and its influence has been long lasting; by 1987 it could be reasonably stated of the post-Franks era that 'over the next quarter century, tribunals pushed increasingly towards a court-substitute function' (Harlow and Rawlings 1997: 393).

With that court-substitute function came an ambition for tribunals similar to that sought for courts: filters to decrease the numbers of appeals. Following the Leggatt Report in 2001 and the emphasis on proportionate dispute resolution in the 2004 White Paper and the transformation of tribunals in 2007, a number of pilots were introduced for informal resolution to be tried before adjudication at hearing. This was the aim, not entirely achieved, of a pilot in 2007–09 to use early neutral evaluation (ENE) in Disability Allowance and Attendance Allowance appeals to the social security tribunal (Hay et al. 2010). Although the pilot did not achieve the time and cost savings hoped for (in fact, the cost of the pilot cases was slightly higher than those that went to hearing), the study found that even for the majority of the cases that proceeded to appeal hearing, benefits of the initial ENE assessment included clearer evidence for the tribunal panel to consider. Less tangible impacts were identified: appellants reported welcoming the chance to talk through their case, and staff reported professional development opportunities and a stronger sense of shared responsibility between the Tribunals Service and the Pension, Disability and Careers Service, which was responsible for initial decision-making. It is easy to see how such intangible benefits might be disregarded in a 'system' that prioritises low cost and efficiency but would be significant gains where participation, collaboration and learning are primary ambitions.

Also with the aim of reducing appeal numbers, administrative or internal review has been introduced in recent years, most notably in the form of Mandatory Reconsideration of benefits decisions. In administrative review the government department making the initial decision carries out a review when its decision is challenged; one policy aim is to provide earlier decisions by avoiding the time for an appeal to tribunal, and the relative low cost of reviews compared to tribunal hearings (£80 for a Mandatory Reconsideration versus nearly £600 for an appeal to the social security tribunal) is clearly part of the mix (Thomas and Tomlinson 2016: 16). Concerns about the quality of administrative review, in which individuals who challenge decisions have little opportunity to participate, and about the effect of 'claimant fatigue' leading to a high attrition rate among potential appellants, suggest that the balance sought between efficiency and quality has not been achieved. The high number of specific categories of appeals upheld, in both the social security and SEND tribunals, suggests there may be limited learning from tribunal decisions and that, to use the language of ombud classification, tribunals do not offer anything more than fire-fighting, and certainly not fire-watching or fire prevention.

What then should a more demosprudential tribunal look like? The national trial in the First-Tier Tribunal SEND, extending the tribunal's power to make recommendations in appeals involving social care and health alongside its binding decisions on education, has been set out above as an example of a more open and networked design. Linking the work of the tribunal and ombuds (such as the SEND Tribunal, the LGSCO, and mediators in SEND) would allow for more opportunity to capture and share learning from these mechanisms, increasing the potential for improving initial decision-making by local authorities and heading off the assembly line of individual complaints that plagues each of them. For individuals, it would mean more impact could be achieved from individual and group complaints, and thus less reliance on individuals to act as enforcers of the law and a fairer reflection of the problems people experience.

The Welsh approach to tribunals, including devolved tribunals on education and mental health, may reflect a distinct way of working that proves to be more demosprudential than currently practiced by tribunals generally. The Committee for Administrative Justice and Tribunals Wales (CAJTW), in its 2016 legacy report, recommended moving away from an adversarial approach to one that is more investigative: 'Wales could take a bold and justifiable leap: it could intentionally recast the devolved tribunals as investigative in principle and practice and thereby create a benchmark for the future of administrative justice in the UK and beyond' (CAJTW 2016: 44). The details of how an investigative tribunal would operate were not set out in the 2017 Wales Act, which otherwise included 'vital legislative reform to the devolved tribunals in Wales which will further encapsulate the concept of an emerging Welsh administrative justice system' (Pritchard 2017).

New technologies hold out both threats and opportunities for tribunals reaching for a place outside Law's Empire. Even within a unified service, tribunals are a disparate group with a range of practices and internal cultures handling nearly half a million appeals each year. As the Senior President of Tribunals has stated, 'there is no 'one size fits all' and each tribunal has its own way of working that is well grounded in the history of its users' needs' (Ryder 2018: 3). Yet for the most part they have been peopled institutions with face-to-face engagement with the public. The ambition for tribunals to be 'digital by default', with various safeguards put in place (such as 'assisted digital'), has been criticised for stripping tribunals of a human element. In initiatives such as hearings by video link, digital justice arguably maintains the human element while reducing obstacles, such as travel costs or inaccessible hearing centres; the London-based Asylum Support Tribunal, for example, uses video links for hearings in asylum cases of claimants dispersed to Glasgow and Belfast (Tomlinson and Thomas 2018: 22). Generally, however, concerns exist (especially among the judiciary) that video links reduce claimants' ability to participate in proceedings and risk the loss of important nonverbal information, such as body language, that can affect consideration of evidence. More concerning is that it has the potential to erode further the relationship between citizen and state. The technological and procedural challenges can no doubt be met, but the human element is hard to replace: 'Democracy's problem is not its inability to synchronise touch-screen inputs and responsive outputs … but its failure to engender relationships of acknowledgement, empathy and respect between representatives and represented' (Design Council 2004: 45).

These relationships can be unpredictable, even messy. Human behaviour is not amenable to design, but Manzini's approach to design for social innovation recognises this in its 'inextricable tangle' of far-reaching vision, giving voice to community, and fostering creativity (Manzini 2015: 62). Social innovation uses technology to coordinate rather than control—to focus 'on people as they are, in all their Kantian crookedness, rather than on how they should be' (Sennett 2018: 163). An example is the way that digitalisation allows for redesigning, and redefining, the concept of 'hearing' in the use of online messaging to facilitate proceedings through ongoing dialogue rather than as a one-off event. Currently being piloted in the First-tier Tribunal (Social Entitlement Chamber) for social security appeals, an online continuous hearing is an inquisitorial and 'an iterative process that takes place over a number of stages which enables the judge and the parties to refine and explore the issues' (Tomlinson and Thomas 2018: 24), as opposed to a one-off in-person hearing that takes place in a physical hearing room in real time. It is a form of social conversation, and the hearing itself becomes a design process in which all actors participate to some degree in shaping the outcome; the decision, or ruling, is the judge's, but the shape that the hearing takes, the toing and froing that forms, ideally, an iterative collaborative process, is one in which all the actors have a role. It is also a process that recognises that 'the user' is in fact many users—individual citizens, public bodies, judges, clerks, legal representatives—and the co-design is one determined by people aided, not controlled, by technology. For some claimants the opportunity it provides to pause, gather evidence, reflect and get advice during a hearing not constrained by real time is a welcome enhancement of access to justice.

Although online continuous hearings illustrate how 'technology can enhance democratic participation by promoting discussion amongst the marginalised and geographically remote' (Mulcahy 2011: 163), retaining design ideals is important if we are to avoid the 'hollowness' of promoting new technologies for the sake of convenience or efficiency (Design Council 2004). In fact, 'democracy may need to be untidy and it may need to operate at less than optimum efficiency' in order to be closer to the citizen (Design Council 2004: 50–51). Physical proximity, the ability to eyeball one another, is one such design ideal and is needed in our cities' public spaces as well as in the places where justice happens: 'those of us who care to retain a strong sense of meaningful accountability should remain sensitive to attempts to undermine the value of physical proximity' (Mulcahy 2011: 176). Face-to-face contact may hold the key to sense-making as part of the design process; certainly, it is 'much more likely to confer interaction with meaning', which is one reason why mediators emphasise the power of face-to-face interaction (Mulcahy 2011: 178).

Public Inquiries: Making Space for Acknowledgement

Similar reservations about legalisation have been expressed in connection with the approach adopted by public inquiries (Blom-Cooper 2017). In its report on setting up and running public inquiries in 2015, welcomed by Lord Woolf and by Sir Robert Francis QC, who had completed the inquiry into the Mid-Staffordshire NHS Foundation Trust in 2013, the Centre for Effective Dispute Resolution (CEDR) pointed out that 'the default style' of many public inquiries, although intended to be inquisitorial, is the adversarial courtroom (CEDR 2015: 68). By contrast, CEDR proposed that traditional courtroom methods of cross-examination should be avoided; that public engagement throughout should be made a priority, including through engagement with groups not just individuals; that space should be made for the expression of emotions, essential in the storytelling that makes up the work of the inquiry; and that recommendations should be carefully followed up, so that the inquiry is able to move the events on for stakeholders by means of a considered and trustworthy process. As Lord Woolf remarked in his Preface, the work of public inquiries contributes to 'public trust in those institutions which are subject to review' as well as to confidence in the inquiry itself (CEDR 2015: 5).

One of the biggest criticisms of public inquiries is that they have not sufficiently involved those who have the deepest interest in the investigation. A recent example takes the issues of trust and confidence into account in the design of the process. In May 2018 the Grenfell Inquiry, chaired by Sir Martin Moore-Bick, began hearings into the 2017 disaster, following initial concern that the inquiry personnel, including its Chair, did not understand or represent the community. Nearly 600 individuals, groups, government bodies and commercial entities have been identified as core participants; this and the amount and scope of the evidence make this an inquiry without precedent, as Moore-Bick has said. The decision to start the inquiry with two weeks of initial 'commemoration hearings', focusing on 'pen portraits' of the victims, signalled a recognition that the victims need to be at the centre of the inquiry and that Grenfell Tower was both a community and a collection of individuals and families with rich lives and stories to tell. This 'humanising effect', brought about with respect and dignity, helps to frame what will be a gruelling search for the truth, for hard facts and for accountability. In closing the Phase 1 hearings in December 2018, Moore-Bick set out the collaborative procedure he proposed for dealing with the request to recommend immediate steps that can be taken in light of the evidence heard in Phase 1, without having to wait for the Phase 1 report. This procedure adopts elements that are found in public interest litigation in India, as set out in Chap. 6, by inviting proposals from core participants and canvassing the views of all participants as well as expert witnesses. The inquiry has also acted on the concerns expressed by participants about the venue for the hearings and identified a location close to the North Kensington site of Grenfell—both a symbolically important measure and one recognising the pragmatic needs of the community to be involved.

The Grenfell inquiry has been deliberately designed to learn the lessons from Hillsborough and to respond to doubts about the integrity of the process (Scraton 2013). In '*The legacy of Hillsborough: liberating truth, challenging power*', Scraton writes about the 'view from below', the alternative accounts (of bereaved families and survivors) that were hidden by the official discourse about Hillsborough. What is needed, he argues, is acknowledgement. Giving space for emotion is one form of acknowledgement. Sennett describes the aftermath of the Grenfell fire as an illustration of authorities and residents speaking different languages—on the one hand, planners explaining the decisions behind the renovation that led to installation of the cladding, and on the other, victims and members of the community wanting acknowledgement of their trauma—widening what he calls the recognition gap. He believes that a genuine process of co-production at the start of the renovation could have prevented the tragedy (Sennett 2018: 263). Whether that is true or not, what he describes could apply as well to the aftermath of an ombud investigation, if the ombud is able to bridge the recognition gap that exists between the complainant and the wider community, on the one hand, and the public body on the other. Even if this leaves space for ambiguity and some dissatisfaction, it is a more democratic, and more truthful, kind of approach.

Super-Complaints: Collective and Networked Accountability

One mechanism for achieving collective and networked accountability—and one that would help mitigate the lack of own-initiative powers of the public sector ombuds in England and the Parliamentary Ombudsman—is the super-complaint. 'Super-complaint' is a concept introduced in the Enterprise Act 2002 as a mechanism for addressing systemic consumer detriment resulting from the conduct or structure of consumer markets. It allows for a designated body, such as a consumer representation body, to initiate a complaint on behalf of a group or groups of individuals with the aim of triggering an investigation, enforcement action, sanctions, voluntary changes, and regulatory action by government. It is not intended to replace existing complaints procedures but to address areas of potential systemic problems that are unlikely to be raised in individual complaints. The concept has been extended to complaints about the financial services market and, more relevant to our purposes, to complaints about police conduct, enabling bodies designated by the Home Secretary to raise super-complaints about actions by all police forces in England and Wales, the National Crime Agency, the Ministry of Defence Police, the Civil Nuclear Constabulary and the British Transport Police. Complaints are considered by a panel including the Independent Office of Police Conduct, the ombud for police complaints.

Elements of the super-complaint reflect the public interest litigation procedure in India's supreme court as described by Fredman (2008) and discussed in Chap. 6. With advice agencies and other NGOs acting as 'role-literate participants' and raising citizens' concerns, and with the ombud adopting fact-finding and deliberative processes and, together with relevant regulators, engaging in iterative shared endeavours, the potential is for the super-complaint concept to ensure that 'those whose voices are drowned in the political melee are given full and equal participation rights' (Fredman 2008: 125). The role of the designated body raising the super-complaint is not as a representative, not 'speaking for others' but 'speaking with others', to frame complaints so that they 'open up areas of conversation which the ordinary paths of "legality" bypass and negate' (Fredman 2008: 140). Concerns about using a super-complaint process in ombud complaints are that the process of designating 'role-literate participant' bodies can be overly bureaucratic and politically charged, triggering territorial and ideological battles between NGOs. These concerns may be overstated: it is not impossible to set out public interest criteria for approving designated bodies, as the Police Super-complaints Regulations 2018 do. Fear of politicisation of the process betrays an unjustifiable concern that ombuds should be considered to stand outside the political arena, a stance that is increasingly unrealistic in the contexts of the austerity agenda pursued by successive UK governments and its resulting strains in individuals and on public services. As Mick King, Local Government and Social Care Ombudsman, described powerfully at the Ombudsman Association annual conference in 2018, ombuds are now operating in a much more politicised space, exemplified by the use of rationing and outsourcing by public bodies and by concerns about homelessness, social care and benefit sanctions being raised in Parliament—'the stakes are raised considerably' (King 2018).

A report by the National Audit Office on the Windrush scandal noted that although concerns had been raised for some years, no overall picture emerged until the media reported on a number of people originally from the Commonwealth who were invited to work and live in Britain in the 1950s and 1960s, or in many cases their children. The stories being reported described people who had lived for decades in the UK, often working in the public sector, being detained in immigration centres and even being deported. Most did not have, or could not access, the necessary paperwork to prove their right to live and work in the UK. Four years before these media stories appeared, the Legal Action Group reported on significant concerns about the impact of the 'compliant environment' policy (otherwise known as the 'hostile environment' policy) on groups of Jamaicans who had arrived before 1973. The NAO concluded that there were warning signs from a number of sources over a long period that were sufficient cumulatively to indicate a potential problem meriting further investigation (NAO 2018: 10). It is worth considering whether, had a super-complaint been an option, NGOs who were seeing clients with these problems might have been able to bring this to the Parliamentary Ombudsman's attention earlier on.

Problems of Prioritising Speed and 'The User'

Working in a more connected way as part of a network, and including within that network designated bodies from civil society, is not seamless or speedy and so presents a challenge to the fast resolution that has become a mantra for reform of administrative justice. The Senior President of

Tribunals has described the 'hallmark' of the tribunals service as the ability to make decisions in ways that are 'informal, flexible and swift' (Ryder 2018: 3). The inquiry process is a reminder that speed is not always the appropriate ambition. Sennett writes of our desire for speed being 'a historical construction of our sensibilities' (Sennett 2018: 36), one linked with ideas of modernity (and today, with expectations tied to the way we communicate through email and social media). 'The experience of street-speed', he writes, 'defines a certain version of modernity: fast is free, slow is unfree' (Sennett 2018: 37). He likens today's Googleplex, the workplaces of Google employees, to the model village of Port Sunlight—a 'classic company town' that 'ties a tight knot between working and dwelling'. All Googleplexi across the globe act as gated communities—they provide 24-hour access to all services and leisure inside the building, to lessen the need for employees to interact with the outside world and get distracted from work. Those who commute into work are transported on company buses with wifi, to ensure the work never stops. The Googleplex, he writes, 'is in the city but not of it' (Sennett 2018: 149).

Part of the problem, Sennett suggests, is that in our desire for speed we expect frictionless exchanges. The term 'friction-free' is used to denote technology that is user friendly, although its workings and mechanics are kept inaccessible—the smartphone or the computerised car, for example. The idea is to design out the 'seams' so that they are invisible to the user. But 'technical paradoxes' arise from this, Sennett says: including over-featuring, the layering on of functions and features, and the resulting lack of understanding in the user. There is a dumbing down inherent in making everything friction-free, complete, non-difficult. What the institutions of administrative justice should aspire to, instead of a mechanistic seamless system whose cogs are well oiled, is a bit of grit, some resistance. Resistance makes us think (Sennett 2018: 151). In this way, a network provides a better model, one that credits the institutions and individuals within it to work things out.

Encounters are of different relational intensities, which Manzini describes as being either high-intensity relationship, which is 'as involving and deep as it is demanding and, ultimately, risky' (because it exposes vulnerability), or low-intensity relationship, a more formalised and predictable interaction. The first, a 'relational encounter', requires commitment, trust and some degree of intimacy; the latter, an 'experiential encounter', is more transactional and is reflected in, for example, the delivery of services, with clear expectations of the people involved (Manzini 2015:

103–104). In the context of citizen grievance, relationships are asymmetrical: litigants and complainants invest a huge amount of commitment, trust and hope in their interaction and expect the same in return. Institutional actors, the operators and service providers, on the other hand, are more likely to see engagement with users as transactional, with limited commitment required in terms of trust and emotional exposure. The vulnerability and the expectations are thus one-sided, perhaps leading to the vociferous sense of outrage expressed by many campaigning groups on behalf of users that the justice system (the court, the ombud) has let them down.

Manzini's framework of 'design for social innovation' addresses this relationship asymmetry by offering 'users' a prominent role but as communities rather than as individual consumers. His approach is a counter to the 'big-ego design' approach that was a legacy 'from the last century's demiurgic vision, in which design was the act of particularly gifted individuals capable of imprinting their personal stamp on artifacts and environments' (Manzini 2015: 66). Instead, design for social innovation prioritises 'dialogic collaboration', with all participants, user and designer alike, able to listen, to change their minds, 'a conversation in which listening is as important as speaking (because it enables interlocutors to understand and empathize with a different point of view and, on this basis, search for solutions)' (Manzini 2015: 67). A designer in this sense is a facilitator of change, a 'midwife', not a nurse or a doctor (Manzini 2015: 69).

It would be naïve to suppose that either enhanced technology or indeed notions of enhanced 'participation' are a panacea, or that either can serve only the common good. The internet and increased connectivity bring risk as well as benefit: not just actual threats of harm (online bullying, financial fraud) but the loss of human, face-to-face interaction. The shift from the early days of the internet and its vision of decentralized power to what is today a concentration of power in the hands of a few state and non-state actors forces us to remain vigilant of connectivity and whom it benefits. Far from serving the values of 'community', 'network' and 'openness', such technologies, if void of good design, can in fact serve the interest of malign closure and isolation. As Sennett has remarked, 'The cities we live in today are closed in ways that mirror what has happened in the tech realm': they inculcate a fear of others and an inability to cope with messiness and human complexity (Sennett 2018).

Nor is the idealisation of 'participation' without its critics. On the contrary, it has been argued forcefully that a focus on participation and co-design, fuelled by a desire to cut costs and expend with experts and infrastructure, can readily serve a neoliberal, consumerist, and small-government ideology, as 'an extension of the choice/consumerism paradigm' (see, e.g., Harris 2018: 27). There is a danger of participation being linked with a 'predatory spirit of neoliberalism' (Baiocchi and Ganuza 2017) and the do-it-yourself culture—the consumerist approach and also the underpinning ethos of ADR as empowering. Such critique is a salutary reminder of the need for vigilance and for the importance of self-conscious 'design', or indeed 'non-design'.

* * *

This chapter has attempted to explore how a more community-focused, open and networked approach might be expanded from the ombud across a wider demosprudential administrative justice fabric. The themes of looking, listening and touching are integral to this vision. As Danielle Allen has suggested, the role of institutions and their ability to foster political friendship is dependent on how people interact; institutions are not 'the other' but are instead 'extensions of our selves' (Allen 2004: 172). Institutions cannot resolve on their own the problem of giving the law too much credit for securing social bonds, which we do, according to Allen, if we think there is only one kind of self-interest (a rivalrous one) and that legal systems are what we need to manage that. The 'institutions' of administrative justice reimagined include new mediation practices that focus on recognition and reciprocity rather than resolution, inquiries that adopt participative processes in which many voices can be heard, and tribunals that openly link with other mechanisms and institutions to facilitate more sustainable, collaborative and collective outcomes rather than maintaining an assembly line of appeals. The following chapter, by way of conclusion, builds on the ideas of political friendship and human capability to explore the political dimensions of a reimagined social rights and administrative justice.

References

Allen, D. (2004). *Talking to Strangers: Anxieties of Citizenship since Brown v. Board of Education*. Chicago: University of Chicago Press.

Baiocchi, G., & Ganuza, E. (2017). Popular Democracy. Blog debate on Centre for Urban Research on Austerity.

Blom-Cooper, L. (2017). *Public Inquiries: Wrong Route on Bloody Sunday*. Oxford: Hart Bloomsbury.

Bondy, V., & Doyle, M. (2011). *Mediation in Judicial Review: A Practical Handbook for Lawyers*. London: Public Law Project.

Bondy, V., Doyle, M., & Reid, V. (2005). Mediation and Judicial Review—Mind the Research Gap. *Judicial Review, 10*(3), 220–226.

Bush, R. A. B., & Folger, J. P. (2005). *The Promise of Mediation: The Transformative Approach to Conflict*. San Francisco: Jossey-Bass.

Centre for Effective Dispute Resolution (CEDR). (2003). *ADR for Public Authorities: A Guide for Managers*. London: CEDR.

Centre for Effective Dispute Resolution (CEDR). (2015). *Setting Up and Running a Public Inquiry: Guidance for Chairs and Commissioning Bodies*. London: CEDR.

Committee for Administrative Justice and Tribunals Wales (CAJTW). (2016). *Legacy Report*. Cardiff: Welsh Assembly.

Department for Education. (2018). Statements of SEN and EHC Plans, England, SFR May 2018. Retrieved February 27, 2019, from https://assets.publishing.service.gov.uk/government/uploads/system/uploads/attachment_data/file/709590/Statements_of_SEN_and_EHC_plans_England_2018_Main_Text.pdf

Design Council. (2004). *Touching the State: What Does It Mean to Be a Citizen in the 21st Century?* London: Design Council and Institute for Public Policy Research.

Doyle, M., Bondy, V., & Hirst, C. (2014). *The Use of Informal Resolution Approaches by Ombudsmen in the UK and Ireland: A Mapping Study*. London: Nuffield Foundation.

Drewry, G. (2009). The Judicialisation of 'Administrative' Tribunals in the UK: From Hewart to Legatt. *Transylvanian Review of Administrative Sciences, 28*, 45–64.

Enterkin, J., & Sefton, M. (2006). *A Report on the Exeter Small Claims Mediation Pilot* (DCA Research Series 10/06). London: Department for Constitutional Affairs.

Fredman, S. (2008). *Human Rights Transformed: Positive Rights and Positive Duties*. Oxford: OUP.

Genn, H., et al. (2007). *Twisting Arms: Court Referred and Court Linked Mediation Under Judicial Pressure* (Research Series 1/07). London: Ministry of Justice.

Gilad, S. (2008). Accountability or Expectations Management? The Role of the Ombudsman in Financial Regulation. *Law & Policy, 30*(2), 227–253.

Harlow, C., & Rawlings, R. (1997). *Law and Administration* (2nd ed.). London: Butterworths.

Harris, N. (2018). Autonomy, Rights and Children with Special Needs: A New Paradigm? Working Paper 2. *Legislative and Policy Developments in Special Educational Needs in England and Additional Support Needs in Scotland: Advancing Children and Young People's Rights*. Edinburgh and Manchester: Universities of Edinburgh and Manchester.

Hay, C., McKenna, K., & Buck, T. (2010). *Evaluation of Early Neutral Evaluation Alternative Dispute Resolution in the Social Security and Child Support Tribunal* (Ministry of Justice Research Series 2/10). London: Ministry of Justice.

Herring, J. (2017). Compassion, Ethics of Care and Legal Rights. *International Journal of Law in Context, 13*(2), 158–171.

King, M. (2018). *Speech to the Annual Conference of the Ombudsman Association*. Edinburgh.

Local Government Ombudsman (LGO). (2014). *Special Educational Needs: Preparing for the Future*. London: LGO.

Local Government and Social Care Ombudsman (LGSCO). (2017). *Education, Health and Care Plans: Our First 100 Investigations*. London: LGSCO.

Mae Architects. (2014). *Places for Strangers: Ideas for Places, People and the City* (S. Bose, Ed.). Zurich: Park Books.

Manzini, E. (2015). *Design, When Everybody Designs: An Introduction to Design for Social Innovation*. Cambridge, MA: MIT Press.

Menkel-Meadow, C. (2002). When Litigation is Not the Only Way: Consensus Building and Mediation as Public Interest Lawyering. *Washington University Journal of Law and Policy, 10*, 37–62.

Menkel-Meadow, C. (2016). *Mediation and Its Applications for Good Decision-Making and Dispute Resolution* (K. U. Leuven, Ed.). Cambridge: Intersentia Ltd.

Ministry of Justice. (2017). SEND Appeal Rates 2014–2017. SEND Tribunal Tables: Statistics on the Appeal Rate to the SEND Tribunal.

Mulcahy, L. (2011). *Legal Architecture: Justice, Due Process and the Place of Law*. London: Routledge.

National Audit Office. (2018). *Handling of the Windrush Situation*. HC 1622 Session 2017–2019. London: National Audit Office.

Office of the Independent Adjudicator (OIA). (2013). *Mediation—A Guide for Students*. Reading: OIA.

Pearce, B., & Stubbs, M. (2000). The Role of Mediation in the Settlement of Planning Disputes at Appeal: The Debate and Research Agenda. *Environment and Planning, 32*, 1335–1358.

Pritchard, H. (2017). Tribunal Reform in Wales under the Wales Act 2017. *UK Administrative Justice Institute (UKAJI)* blog.

Ryder, E. (2018). *The Modernisation of Tribunals 2018: A Report by the Senior President of Tribunals*. London: HMCTS.

Scottish Government. (2009). *A Guide to the Use of Mediation in the Planning System in Scotland*. Edinburgh: Scottish Government.

Scraton, P. (2013). The Legacy of Hillsborough: liberating Truth, Challenging Power. *Race & Class, 55*(2), 1–27.

Sennett, R. (2018). *Building and Dwelling*. London: Allen Lane.

Thomas, R., & Tomlinson, J. (2016). *Current Issues in Administrative Justice: Examining Administrative Review, Better Initial Decisions, and Tribunal Reform*. Sheffield and Manchester: Universities of Sheffield and Manchester.

Tomlinson, J., & Thomas, R. (2018). *The Digitalisation of Tribunals: What We Know and What We Need to Know*. London: Public Law Project and UK Administrative Justice Institute.

CHAPTER 8

The Politics of Administrative Justice

Abstract This chapter concludes by considering the political implications of administrative justice reimagined. It does so by returning to the centrality of relationships for administrative justice, and in particular the relationship between citizen and state. The chapter proposes that administrative justice reimagined is unavoidably implicated in the prioritisation of democratic values and equality. It finds in the Aristotelian concept of 'political friendship' the establishment of administrative justice as a set of 'bridging institutions' that are supportive of human capability, social innovation and networked governance. It proposes that the realliance of administrative justice and human rights in the small places of daily life is one way of revitalising for a new digitalised era a post-war vision of social citizenship.

Keywords Political friendship • Social innovation • Human capability • Networked governance • Social citizenship

Administrative Justice is Political

This book has proposed a reimagining of administrative justice, with the ombud institution at its centre. That reimagining has replaced the dominant motifs of individual user, system and closure with community, network and openness. In the process of reimagining, it has become increasingly apparent that this exercise in displacement is unavoidably political in its implications. As soon as administrative justice is reinstated as

M. Doyle, N. O'Brien, *Reimagining Administrative Justice*,
https://doi.org/10.1007/978-3-030-21388-6_8

a set of principles that shapes relationships between citizen and state, it necessarily expresses a political vision. Liberated from its confinement as a 'system' alongside other such justice systems, administrative justice touches the political fabric and fashions its design.

As previous chapters have emphasised, that political context is far from new. The story of administrative justice in its post-war form has from the outset been implicated in political considerations. The narrative of its development is in fact nothing less than the capture of an originally political vision by a narrower set of legal preoccupations. Broad conceptions of democratic citizenship, the public good and virtuous dispositions have given way to concerns about the rule of law, individual libertarian rights and the quality of decision-making. At the same time, the construction of political theory has rarely started at street-level, in the small places where the citizen encounters the state in daily life, in schools, hospitals, benefit offices, and public housing. The gulf between politics and administrative justice has remained unbridged.

Yet as Raymond Williams realised in 1961, if the state is to express in practice its democratic ideals it must do so precisely in those daily transactions that form the staple diet of administrative justice concerns. In the off-hand and superior tone of local authority housing officers in the 1950s and early 1960s Williams detected the survival of pre-democratic mentalities and attitudes that belied the underlying vision of the post-war settlement (Williams 1961). Richard Sennett, describing the encounters of the residents of the Cabrini Green estate with the welfare system in post-war Chicago, highlights too the lack of mutual respect as an expression of a deeply divided society (Sennett 2003). Ken Loach's film, *I, Daniel Blake*, captures vividly, and more recently, the pathos of the individual's struggle with a benefits system infused with the values of the new public management and of a state bureaucracy still devoid of humanising qualities (Laverty and Loach 2016).

More systematically, Bernardo Zacka has shown how a bottom-up approach to political theory, from street to state, powerfully discloses the contours of the relationship between citizen and state. In doing so, he demonstrates how frontline officials and street-level bureaucrats (those working in public service agencies who 'effectively serve as the face of the state for ordinary citizens' (Zacka 2017: 4)) do not merely implement public policy according to some sort of compliance model handed down from above. Instead, through the exercise of surprisingly wide discretion and the expression of deeply ethical dispositions, they shape the implementation of public policy in crucial ways, whilst espousing fundamental values of fairness, efficiency, responsiveness and respect (Zacka 2017).

Zacka argues that despite this value-orientation, street-level bureaucrats are vulnerable to recurring patterns of pathology: the tendency to 'indifference', which creates the classic Weberian and Kafkaesque image of the faceless and unfeeling bureaucrat, preoccupied with process at the expense of any humane considerations; the tendency to 'care giving', whereby sympathy for the individual trumps fairness and so allows sentiment to defeat larger ambitions of social justice; and the tendency to 'enforcement', which creates a shield of zealous rule-compliance whereby the end justifies the means (Zacka 2017).

As forms of resistance to these pathologies, Zacka posits the cultivation of personal virtue and various 'practices of the self' to mitigate the cognitive distortions and stress arising in frontline work, techniques of 'everyday casuistry' (in the sense of pragmatic rationalisation), and a pluralistic suite of accountability mechanisms that encompass what he identifies as hierarchical, direct, professional and peer-level elements. It is in the support of these modes of resistance that administrative justice of the kind described in this book should play a decisive part. By prioritising community, network and openness, administrative justice emerges as a context for reinforcing those resistances and in that way humanising the relationship between the citizen and the state. In doing so, as Zacka demonstrates, administrative justice is inherently political and much more than the anodyne practice of hygienic decision-making.

A challenge is presented to Zacka's portrayal of human decision-making by frontline bureaucrats through the increased use of automated decision-making, which provides 'an incentive for decision-making systems to be designed that emphasise hard-edged rules and reduce or eliminate the capacity of officials to provide personalised solutions' (Le Sueur 2016: 10). Concerns include the lack of transparency, particularly given that many algorithms used by public bodies will be developed by commercial developers with a proprietorial interest in maintaining secrecy; the risk that conscious and unconscious prejudices will be designed into the algorithms; and the inability to challenge the reasons behind automated decisions. It is not just the lack of transparency itself, but also 'explainability or understandability' (Williams 2018: 27); decisions made by algorithm 'might be opaque not only to those who want to challenge it, but even to the human decision-makers previously responsible. It is entirely possible for there to be no accountable human being who understands fully how the decision was reached' (Williams 2018: 24). The answer is not to reject the use of algorithms, which might hold promise of more objective and thus fairer decisions, but to retain scrutiny rather than to be in thrall to technology and its promises of effectiveness and speed. The Cabinet Office and the Information Commissioner have suggested, along the lines proposed by Le Sueur, that some automated decisions should be identified as requiring a level of human oversight and intervention and that other insights should inform the ultimate decision. Where the impact on the individual is significant, the need for human intervention in automated processes becomes more urgent (Williams 2018: 40).

At its core, in any event administrative justice gives expression to political values and to a positive and egalitarian conception of democratic citizenship. This broadly political interpretation of administrative justice is at odds, however, with the socio-legal models that have gained prominence in the recent literature of public administration. It is at odds also with an overly individualistic and libertarian approach to human rights, of the sort to which Samuel Moyn has taken particular exception when he suggests that human rights in the neoliberal era have contributed to material inequality (Moyn 2018).

As mentioned earlier, in 1983 Jerry Mashaw proposed an influential account of administrative justice as the incidence of justice experienced at each stage of a decision-making process that reaches from the first-instance decision-making of street-level bureaucrats to the rulings of the highest courts on appeal. At each of these stages there is a compromise or 'trade-off' between different models of decision-making characterised by normative criteria that are variously bureaucratic, legalistic or professional (Mashaw 1983). More recently, in 2003 and 2006, Michael Adler, has added three more models, associated respectively with managerialism, consumerism and the market (Adler 2003, 2006).

In the terms adopted in this book, each of these models, notwithstanding their surface differences, expresses an essentially jurisprudential mentality, governed by dominant values of individual user, system and closure as the marks of tidy and fair decision-making. The imaginative context is that of the individual case, landing on the desk of a decision-maker and inviting resolution, within carefully prescribed systematic limits, albeit informed by preferences in the margins that may betray the dominance of one or other of the normative models advanced. In each instance what is lacking is any preference for the public good, for the interconnection of accountability agencies and for iterative processes that are open, participatory and susceptible to deliberative approaches. To that extent, socio-legal models of this sort are prefatory to an individualistic ethos and a neoliberal politics that is in tension with the relational and demosprudential vision advanced in this book.

Similarly, as Moyn has shown, the political trajectory of human rights as they have developed since the early phase of the post-war period has been towards an individualistic and neoliberal form that finds little place for social or relational rights, or for methods of 'enforcement' that are not formally adjudicative (Moyn 2018). Insofar as human rights can be construed as an attempt to infuse the legal with the political (Schiavone 2012), they have to some extent become a vehicle for the transposition of merely neoliberal values.

On this account, as outlined in this book, both administrative justice and human rights, whilst inherently and unavoidably political, have unwittingly found themselves in allied propagation of an individualistic and market-oriented ethic that has become the default position of liberal democracies since the 1970s. That default position now faces new challenges, not least since the financial collapse of 2008 and the rise of populist movements in Europe and America, especially since 2016. The reimagining of the alliance between administrative justice and human rights, stripped of their neoliberal accretions, brings with it, therefore, a political vision. What then are the chief components of such a vision yielded by the account of administrative justice offered in this book and that might sustain this imaginative exercise in political practice?

The Bridges of Political Friendship

Various motifs have recurred throughout this book. Apart from the repeated emphasis on community, network and openness, the discussion has consistently been drawn to images of attentiveness, of looking, listening or even touching; to signs of openness and the transgression of settled boundaries; to practices that are more than merely consultative but actively deliberative and participatory. Above all, the discussion has returned to the centrality of democratic values and equality, and of administrative justice and human rights as expressions of these values. To that extent, the argument has affirmed liberal and democratic ideals: its reimagining is framed by the possibilities of liberal democracy and the freedoms it has won, especially for oppressed groups.

At the same time, the discussion has yielded a tension between that vision and the broader communitarian aspirations that lay at the social democratic origins of both administrative justice and human rights and that have been highlighted by the soundings taken in the history of design culture. The identification of that tension invites a measure of rebalancing, so that the 'democratic' and 'liberal' components of liberal democracy are given at least equal weight, even to the extent that the 'liberal' is recognised as a means to, or aspect of, the 'democratic'.

In this context, 'democratic' carries with it a strong emphasis on the primacy of 'equality' as its informing value and a recognition that democracy, even when 'liberal', is also inherently 'social'. It is no accident therefore that the reimagining of administrative justice, in alliance with the human rights of small places, finds its origins and inspiration in that postwar social-democratic moment.

A democratic vision of human rights is a vision of the ordinary, the routine, the obscure and the banal—Eleanor Roosevelt's prescription of human rights for small places, scarcely visible on the map of the world. It is a vision, also, that is familiar to Daniel Blake and the millions like him (O'Brien 2017). It is fundamentally a vision whose conception of citizenship is one that Danielle Allen has referred to as an instance of Aristotelian 'political friendship'. In this context, the place of law is unremittingly demosprudential, 'a practice in which any and every citizen may be involved at any moment, through deliberation, legislation or enforcement … As citizens deal with contingencies attendant on law's enforcement, they renegotiate loss and sacrifice constantly. This is the core activity of the practice of law' (Allen 2004: 170; Ramesh 2013).

For Allen, political friendship, unlike personal friendship which rests on personal 'bonds', depends on the construction of political 'bridges', which in turn make possible the maintenance of trust. 'Trust cultivation' and the practice of negotiating loss that goes with it become a central component of civic virtue, facilitated by the successful operation of 'bridging' institutions that enable also the negotiation of difference. The objective, according to Allen, is 'the connected society' in which social competence at establishing bridging relationships entails better problem-solving in ways which are compatible with diversity and not dependent on social homogeneity. In that way, institutional architecture of this sort challenges the view, expressed for example by David Goodhart, that there is a limit to how much diversity a society can tolerate, whether, between racial and ethnic groups, or other cultural interests such as those he describes as 'Somewheres' and 'Anywheres' (Goodhart 2017).

On this account, administrative justice can be seen as a series of 'bridging institutions' whose 'habits' of trust and public virtue are enhanced by design principles and operational practices that in turn are animated by human rights values and principles. As recent collaboration in Northern Ireland between the Ombudsman and the Human Rights Commission has shown, the practices of administrative justice can be significantly enhanced by the application of the abiding human rights principles of Fairness, Respect, Equality, Dignity and Autonomy (Northern Ireland Ombudsman 2016).

That 'trust' in public institutions is more generally in short supply has been articulated by public philosophers (O'Neill 2018) and further demonstrated by recent socio-legal research on the ombud as presently conceived. Studies in Belgium, the Netherlands and the UK have found, for example, that at present ombud-institutions have 'no noticeable effect in helping people trust the government' and that usually only a distinct, socially advantaged group make use of ombuds in the first place (Creutzfeldt 2016: 460; Hertogh 2013). As Naomi Creutzfeldt has remarked, 'The mismatch between users' expectations and what institutions of accountability can deliver creates a rupture in the trust relationship' (Creutzfeldt 2016: 466). As Creutzfeldt also suggests, however, an important part of that mismatch arises from the way in which public expectation of the ombud is shaped by national preconceptions drawn from legal consciousness. What people expect from an ombud, and no doubt from administrative justice, is judged against the standard of the judicial process. Insofar as non-legalistic administrative justice waits to be reclaimed as 'an overarching set of principles and values' that might replenish that deficit and heal that rupture, then an effective resource lies ready to hand in the reclamation from neoliberalism of that body of social and relational values and principles developed since the Second World War and known quite simply as 'human rights'.

Yet to be effective, such a resource will in this context need to avoid being hijacked not only by the purveyors of 'law' but of 'sentiment' as ethical foundation, the rigorously remote application of unbending rules on the one hand, or the deliciously personal prescription of 'love is all you need' on the other. In the world of Daniel Blake, neither benevolent 'customer service' nor 'objective' rule-adherence by impersonal 'decision-maker' is likely to prove a viable remedy to the depicted experience of corrosive dehumanisation. The more complex terrain of Aristotelian 'friendship' remains a richer, albeit less easily mapped, route to the good society, the construction of habits of trust its defining feature. 'Administrative justice' is, in the end, one of the names we have for that ethically-political activity, 'human rights' the name for that 'still far from complete process of the integration of politics into law…unknown to the ancient world, [but] from which modern democracy took form' (Schiavone 2012: 458).

As literary and political theorist Terry Eagleton has remarked in his own extended reflection on 'trouble with strangers', the relation 'between ethics and politics does not turn on a contrast between love and administration, the infinite and the finite, the near and the far, intimates and strangers or the asymmetrical and the symmetrical…The ethical is a matter of how we may live with each other most rewardingly, whilst the political is a question of what institutions will best promote this end' (Eagleton 2009: 324–325). In the realm of administrative justice, the practical implications of such a philosophy of institutions, the good life and the good society are clear: that the evaluation of the work of public authorities, including their provision of public 'services', should not be preoccupied exclusively with 'customer care' and 'customer satisfaction' but with the establishment of deeper and more durable relationships of trust; that the response to citizen grievance should not be reduced to remote and unyielding forms of individual 'dispute resolution' without regard to shared and structural considerations; that tribunals, public inquiries and ombud-institutions should not be so colonised by Law's Empire that they become mere imitations of judicial process and thereby squander their potentially distinctive contribution to the 'cult of bureaucratic humanity'.

The active state, as recognised by William Morris Jones in the social democratic post-war moment, can hardly escape 'the problem of bureaucracy' altogether: retreat to pre-bureaucratic familial, religious and charitable provision is not a just alternative. The humanisation of state bureaucracy and the restoration of trust remain, however, a realisable goal and, in the light of the administrative justice and human rights tragedy which is Grenfell Tower, one whose realisation is demonstrably urgent. The reimagining of administrative justice as an agent of that institutional reform, of public trust, human rights and a 'connected society' is not a utopian dream but a practical necessity.

Social Innovation and Networked Governance

It has been the contention of this book that in facing this challenge administrative justice and human rights do not stand alone. Instead they share a broader cultural context from which inspiration may be drawn. The vulnerability of administrative justice and human rights to the pathology of legalism has been detected across the cultural sphere and in particular in the design-wars between individual and community, system and network, closure and openness. Those tensions are now all the more acute as a result of technological development and the aspiration in public policy that reform initiatives, including within the justice 'system', be 'digital by default'. It is trite to observe that such technological development brings in its wake both opportunity and risk. On the deficit side, there is the spectre of even further dehumanisation, isolation and exclusion; on the credit side, the prospect of unparalleled fulfilment, connectivity and inclusion.

If administrative justice, in harness with relational and social human rights, is to be a source of credit, not deficit, it will need to embrace the tenets not so much of 'new' governance but of 'networked' governance. If bottom-up initiatives are to be released from their bureaucratic shackles, top-down governance structures will need to become enabling factors. In this context, governance is nothing less than 'the management of public power, the production of the public sphere, and ultimately…the way the state and its agencies interact with its citizens and their organisations' (Manzini 2015: 157). Technological innovation has in turn become the means by which new ways of interaction between people is made possible.

The story of the transformation of old-style 'command-and-control' governance by 'new governance' is by now familiar. Central to that story is the way in which models of management devised in the private sector were translated in the 1980s and 1990s to the public sector in the development of what became known as 'the new public management'. The epilogue to the story of new public management is one in which its principles have in turn been subject to modernising critique. That critique is based in particular on the tendency for new public management to characterise the individual person as passive, isolated and disembodied, rather than as an active, social and embedded subject capable of taking a deliberative part in the creation of the public good (Manzini 2015: 158). The latter designation of human potential entails the positive recognition that such engaged subjects create collaborative organisations, which in turn should become the cornerstone of networked governance. As the mission statement of a design agency founded in 2007 puts it, 'We believe there needs to be a new settlement between individuals, communities and government—new ways for people to get involved in determining their lives in a meaningful way, new approaches that mean some people do not get stuck at the bottom of the heap for generations and new bonds that mean people can flourish and bring their dreams alive' (Manzini 2015: 159).

As noted above, in the case of administrative justice the aspiration should be not so much the creation of familiar bonds between like-minded folk but the establishment of viable bridges between citizens whose difference is their strength. In that endeavour, the state is complicit and, in its remaking of the relationship between citizen and state, the administrative justice of small places is complicit also. Whatever formulation prevails, whether 'partner state', 'relational state', or 'relational welfare', networked governance depends on connectivity, horizontal styles of decision-making, knowledge exchange and dialogue (Manzini 2015: 159). This reimagining of governance in turn provides the basis for a 'new vision of the relationship between citizens and state: a vision in which ordinary people become not only co-designers but also co-producers of a new public space in which… "the state becomes a partner state": a state that actively supports its citizens, through its agencies and policies, in the conception and realization of their life projects' (Manzini 2015: 160).

Underpinning such aspirations is the recognition that the 'users' of public services should no longer be considered 'people with problems' but instead as co-producers, 'people with capabilities'. Human well-being on this account is not dependent on personal characteristic or the satisfaction of need by material possessions, so much as on the possibility of acting and making use of those goods or characteristics. In the theory of human capability developed by Martha Nussbaum, 'capabilities' are people's abilities to choose between alternatives and achieve positive 'functionings', such as being adequately fed, housed and clothed, being able to meet friends and have relationships with them, being able to live freely and without public shame, being able to communicate and participate and follow one's own creative instincts (Nussbaum 2011).

The prescriptions of human capability theory are an antidote to, or refinement of, what Richard Sennett identifies as the three abiding 'codes of respect' in modern society, the three primary means by which citizens achieve self-respect and the respect of others. Those codes of respect are, first, 'make something of yourself'; secondly, 'take care of yourself'; and thirdly, 'help others'. Yet as Sennett observes, each of these apparently straightforward codes is fatally undermined or, as he puts it, 'tarnished', by the perennial spectre of inequality. Sennett's remedy is to nuance these respective codes by honouring the diversity of practical achievements rather than privileging potential talent; by admitting the just claims of adult dependency, even when everything has been done that can be done in the name of autonomy; and by permitting people to participate more actively in the conditions of their own 'care'. His conclusion follows: 'each of these principles has a concrete application in the welfare system; all three would increase rather than make more scarce mutual respect between doctors and patients, the managers and residents of public housing, and social workers and their clients' (Sennett 2003: 261).

* * *

The cumulative force of the interlocking insights derived in this chapter from the work of Danielle Allen, Ezio Manzini, Martha Nussbaum, and Richard Sennett point, by way of conclusion, to a form of politics in which the value of equality is a necessary counter-balance to the celebration of negative liberty. Upon the foundation of equality is built the positive freedom to achieve shared human potential rather than merely the enjoyment of individual freedom from state interference. As such, it is a politics that entails a positive appreciation of the state and of the relationships that citizens are enabled to forge with the state and with each other. Political friendship, social innovation, human capability and mutual respect are on this account the watchwords of active social citizenship. They are the watchwords also of administrative justice reimagined in the small places of relational and social human-rights, and as an essential component of a democracy that, in a digital age, is not merely deliberative but both egalitarian and participatory (Allen and Light 2015).

This book started with the social democratic moment of the post-war period, and it will end there also. When T.H. Marshall delivered the lectures in Cambridge in 1949 that would emerge in classic published form in 1950 as *Citizenship and Social Class* (Marshall 1992), his concern was not merely with the welfare state as a means of eradicating social destitution but of enabling social equality as well. As Samuel Moyn has emphasised, Marshall, more than other contemporary commentators, provides an indicator of how the 'egalitarian ambience of social rights' is critical to understanding the character of the post-war era and of how much has changed since. Distributive equality, as much as sufficiency, was to be the legacy of the new welfare state. To that extent, social rights 'did breathe the materially egalitarian spirit of their moment' and were an important advance on the libertarian rights of nineteenth-century political economy (Moyn 2018: 43). It is in this light that the Universal Declaration must be re-read, as 'centrally about distributive justice, not merely the liberties of mind, speech, and person that made "human rights" so prominent decades later'. The Universal Declaration to that extent fits 'snugly in its era as a charter or template for national welfare states and a canonization of some premises of twentieth-century citizenship' (Moyn 2018: 44).

Marshall, in the spirit of the Universal Declaration, insisted that equality is the essence of citizenship and that citizenship—as political ideal rather than legal construction, or, following Danielle Allen, what we might call 'civic agency' (Allen and Light 2015)—entails equality of respect and the satisfaction of material need, not merely basic provision. The social rights entailed by civic agency, as much as by the Universal Declaration, were about local communities and their active, participatory restoration, rather than global surveillance. On this account, the welfare state was to be a 'talisman against the geopolitics of war, not some supranational authority for a politics of atrocity prevention abroad'. As a result, it comes as a shock for 'newcomers to the document in a neoliberal age' to find the focus on the 'modular reproduction of the welfare state, not the founding of the global project of monitoring despots for the worst abuses and genocidal violence before all else' (Moyn 2018: 44).

The Universal Declaration is, in other words, above all else, and as Eleanor Roosevelt spelt out in simple terms, a charter for the relational social human rights of small places. Administrative justice is nothing less than the form of demosprudential and networked governance available in the twenty-first century for the realisation of these social human rights. That such realisation entails a measure of reimagining has been the theme of this book. It is quite simply in the small places of administrative justice, on the streets, close to home, that the citizen meets the state and where the possibilities of political friendship may be both signified and made real.

References

Adler, M. (2003). A Socio-Legal Approach to Administrative Justice. *Law and Policy, 25*(4), 323–352.

Adler, M. (2006). Fairness in Context. *Journal of Law and Society, 33*(4), 615–638.

Allen, D. (2004). *Talking to Strangers: Anxieties of Citizenship since Brown v. Board of Education*. Chicago: University of Chicago Press.
Allen, D., & Light, J. (Eds.). (2015). *From Voice to Influence*. Chicago: University of Chicago Press.
Creutzfeldt, N. (2016). A Voice for Change? Trust Relationships between Ombudsmen, Individuals and Public Service Providers. *Journal of Social Welfare and Family Law, 38*, 460–479.
Eagleton, T. (2009). *Trouble with Strangers*. Oxford: Wiley-Blackwell.
Goodhart, D. (2017). *The Road to Somewhere: The Populist Revolt and the Future of Politics*. London: C Hurst & Co.
Hertogh, M. (2013). Why the Ombudsman Does Not Promote Public Trust in Government: Lessons from the Low Countries. *Journal of Social Welfare and Family Law, 35*, 245–258.
Laverty, P., & Loach, K. (2016). *I, Daniel Blake*. Pontefract: Route Publishing.
Le Sueur, A. (2016). Robot Government: Automated Decision-Making and Its Implications for Parliament. In A. Horne & A. Le Sueur (Eds.), *Parliament: Legislation and Accountability*. Oxford: Hart Publishing.
Manzini, E. (2015). *Design, When Everybody Designs: An Introduction to Design for Social Innovation*. Cambridge, MA: MIT Press.
Marshall, T. H. (1992). Citizenship and Social Class. In T. H. Marshall & T. Bottomore (Eds.), *Citizenship and Social Class*. London: Pluto.
Mashaw, J. (1983). *Bureaucratic Justice: Managing Social Security Disability Claims*. New Haven: Yale University Press.
Moyn, S. (2018). *Not Enough: Human Rights in an Unequal World*. Cambridge, MA: Harvard University Press.
Northern Ireland Ombudsman. (2016). *Human Rights Manual*. Belfast: Northern Ireland Ombudsman and Northern Ireland Human Rights Commission.
Nussbaum, M. (2011). *Creating Capabilities: The Human Development Approach*. Cambridge, MA: Harvard University Press.
O'Brien, N. (2017). Administrative Justice in the Wake of 'I, Daniel Blake'. *Political Quarterly, 89*(1), 82–91.
O'Neill, O. (2018). *A Question of Trust: The BBC Reith Lectures 2002*. Cambridge: CUP.
Ramesh, R. (2013, May 1). Equity Not Equality—Interview with Danielle Allen. *The Guardian*, p. 35.
Schiavone, A. (2012). *The Invention of Law in the West*. Cambridge, MA: Harvard.
Sennett, R. (2003). *Respect: The Formation of Character in an Age of Inequality*. New York: W W Norton & Company.
Williams, R. (1961). *The Long Revolution*. London: Chatto and Windus.
Williams, R. (2018). Rethinking Deference for Algorithmic Decision-making. *Oxford Legal Studies Research Paper No. 7/2019*.
Zacka, B. (2017). *When the State Meets the Street: Public Service and Moral Agency*. Cambridge, MA: Harvard University Press.

References

Adler, M. (2003). A Socio-Legal Approach to Administrative Justice. *Law and Policy, 25*(4), 323–352.

Adler, M. (2006). Fairness in Context. *Journal of Law and Society, 33*(4), 615–638.

Adler, M. (Ed.). (2010). *Administrative Justice in Context*. Oxford: Hart.

Adler, M. (2012). The Rise and Fall of Administrative Justice—A Cautionary Tale. *Socio-Legal Review, 8*, 29–54.

Adler, M. (2018). *Cruel, Inhuman or Degrading Treatment: Benefit Sanctions in the UK*. London: Palgrave Pivot.

Administrative Justice and Tribunals Council (AJTC). (2010). *Principles of Administrative Justice*. London: AJTC.

Albers, A. (1965). *On Weaving*. Middletown, CT: Wesleyan University Press.

Allen, D. (2004). *Talking to Strangers: Anxieties of Citizenship since Brown v. Board of Education*. Chicago: University of Chicago Press.

Allen, D., & Light, J. (Eds.). (2015). *From Voice to Influence*. Chicago: University of Chicago Press.

Ambedkar, B. R. (2010). Speech Delivered on 25 November 1949. In B. Das (Ed.), *Thus Spoke Ambedkar*. New Delhi: Navayana Publishing.

Anthony, G. (2015). Administrative Justice in the United Kingdom. *Italian Journal of Public Law, 7*(1), 9–33.

Baiocchi, G., & Ganuza, E. (2017). Popular Democracy. Blog debate on Centre for Urban Research on Austerity.

Barry, G. (1952). The Festival of Britain 1951. *Journal of the Royal Society of Arts, 100*(4880), 667–704.

Ben Jelloun, T. (2016). *By Fire: Writings on the Arab Spring* (R. S. Nezami, Trans.). Evanston, IL: Northwestern University Press.

M. Doyle, N. O'Brien, *Reimagining Administrative Justice*,
https://doi.org/10.1007/978-3-030-21388-6

Berlin, I. (1969). Two Concepts of Liberty. In I. Berlin (Ed.), *Four Essays on Liberty*. Oxford: OUP.
Berman, G., & Feinblatt, J. (2001). *Problem-Solving Courts: A Brief Primer*. New York: Center for Court Innovation.
Blom-Cooper, L. (2017). *Public Inquiries: Wrong Route on Bloody Sunday*. Oxford: Hart Bloomsbury.
Bondy, V., & Doyle, M. (2011). *Mediation in Judicial Review: A Practical Handbook for Lawyers*. London: Public Law Project.
Bondy, V., Doyle, M., & Reid, V. (2005). Mediation and Judicial Review—Mind the Research Gap. *Judicial Review, 10*(3), 220–226.
Bondy, V., & Le Sueur, A. (2012). *Designing Redress: A Study about Grievances against Public Bodies*. London: Public Law Project.
Bondy, V., et al. (2009). *Mediation and Judicial Review: An Empirical Research Study*. London: Public Law Project.
Bondy, V., Platt, L., & Sunkin, M. (2015). *The Value and Effects of Judicial Review: The Nature of Claims, Their Outcomes and Consequences*. London: Public Law Project.
Bondy, V., & Sunkin, M. (2009). *The Dynamics of Judicial Review Litigation: The Resolution of Public Law Challenges before Final Hearing*. London: Public Law Project.
Bonsiepe, G. (2010). *Design and Democracy*. London: Bedford Press.
Bottomore, T. (1992). Citizenship and Social Class, Forty Years On. In T. H. Marshall & T. Bottomore (Eds.), *Citizenship and Social Class*. London: Pluto.
Bracken, M. (2015). Mapping New Ideas for the Digital Justice System. *Government Digital Service* blog.
Breward, C., & Wilcox, C. (2012). *The Ambassador Magazine: Promoting Post-war British Textiles and Fashion*. London: V&A Publishing.
Brown, M. (2018, July 18). V&A's 'Less Scary' Entrance Drives Up Visitor Numbers. *The Guardian*.
Bua, A. (2017). Book Review: Popular Democracy: The Paradox of Participation by Gianpaolo Baiocchi and Ernesto Ganuza. *LSE Review of Books*, LSE Blog.
Buck, T., Kirkham, R., & Thompson, B. (2011). *The Ombudsman Enterprise and Administrative Justice*. Farnham: Ashgate.
Busck, L. (1995). The History and Development of the Institution of Ombudsman. In H. Gammeltoft-Hansen (Ed.), *The Danish Ombudsman*. Copenhagen: The Danish Ombudsman.
Bush, R. A. B., & Folger, J. P. (2005). *The Promise of Mediation: The Transformative Approach to Conflict*. San Francisco: Jossey-Bass.
Cabinet Office. (2010). *Ombudsman Schemes: Guidance for Departments*. London: Cabinet Office.
Cassin, R. (1972). *La Pensee et l'Action*. Boulogne: F Lalou.
Castellani, L. (2017). The Citizen's Charter: Towards Consumer Service in Central Government. *History & Policy*.

Centre for Effective Dispute Resolution (CEDR). (2003). *ADR for Public Authorities: A Guide for Managers*. London: CEDR.
Centre for Effective Dispute Resolution (CEDR). (2015). *Setting Up and Running a Public Inquiry: Guidance for Chairs and Commissioning Bodies*. London: CEDR.
Chayes, A. (1976). The Role of the Judge in Public Law Litigation. *Harvard Law Review*, *89*, 1281–1316.
Cole, T. (2016). *Known and Strange Things*. London: Faber & Faber.
Coleman, S. (2004). Tangible Democracy. In *Touching the State: What Does It Mean to Be a Citizen in the 21st Century?* London: Design Council and Institute for Public Policy Research.
College of Policing, et al. (2018). Police Super-complaints: Guidance on Submitting a Super-complaint about Policing. Retrieved February 18, 2019, from https://www.gov.uk/government/collections/police-super-complaints
Committee for Administrative Justice and Tribunals Wales (CAJTW). (2016). *Legacy Report*. Cardiff: Welsh Assembly.
Constenla, C. (2013). Del Monte Sacro a Salvador de Bahia: Sobre quien podria ser el Defensor del Pueblo. *Revista de la Asociacion de Derecho Administrativo de la Ciudad Autonoma de Buenos Aires*, *5*, 195–208.
Constenla, C. (2014). Defensor del Pueblo: un enemigo del pueblo? *Eforos, Publicacion Semestral del Instituto Latinoamericano del Ombudsman-Defensor del Pueblo*, June–December, 21–30.
Constenla, C. (2015). El Defensor del Pueblo in Latin America. *Visioni Latino-Americane*, *12*, 59–72.
Coverley, M. (2010). *Psychogeography*. Harpenden: Pocket Essentials.
Creutzfeldt, N. (2016). A Voice for Change? Trust Relationships between Ombudsmen, Individuals and Public Service Providers. *Journal of Social Welfare and Family Law*, *38*, 460–479.
Creutzfeldt, N. (2018). *Ombudsmen and ADR: A Comparative Study of Informal Justice in Europe*. Geneva: Palgrave Macmillan.
Crossman, R. (1956). *Socialism and the New Despotism*. London: Fabian Society.
Crowther, N. (2018a). On Economic, Social and Cultural Rights We Need to Look Carefully before We Leap. *Making Rights Make Sense* blog.
Crowther, N. (2018b). Following Grenfell, How Can Human Rights Have Real Meaning in the 'Small Places, Close to Home'? *Making Rights Make Sense* blog.
de Certeau, M. (1984). *The Practice of Everyday Life*. Berkeley: University of California Press.
Department for Education. (2018). Statements of SEN and EHC Plans, England, SFR May 2018. Retrieved February 27, 2019, from https://assets.publishing.service.gov.uk/government/uploads/system/uploads/attachment_data/file/709590/Statements_of_SEN_and_EHC_plans_England_2018_Main_Text.pdf

Design Council. (2004). *Touching the State: What Does It Mean to Be a Citizen in the 21st Century?* London: Design Council and Institute for Public Policy Research.

Design Museum. (2015). Jock Kinneir and Margaret Calvert. London: Design Museum. Retrieved February 18, 2019, from http://designmuseum.org/design/jock-kinneir-margaret-calvert

Dorf, M., & Sabel, C. (1998). A Constitution of Democratic Experimentalism. *Columbia Law Review, 98*, 267–473.

Doyle, M., Bondy, V., & Hirst, C. (2014). *The Use of Informal Resolution Approaches by Ombudsmen in the UK and Ireland: A Mapping Study*. London: Nuffield Foundation.

Drewry, G. (2009). The Judicialisation of 'Administrative' Tribunals in the UK: From Hewart to Legatt. *Transylvanian Review of Administrative Sciences, 28*, 45–64.

Dworkin, R. (1986). *Law's Empire*. London: Fontana.

Eagleton, T. (2009). *Trouble with Strangers*. Oxford: Wiley-Blackwell.

Eakin, E. (2011, October 31). Celluloid Hero. *The New Yorker*.

Elkin, L. (2016). *Flaneuse: Women Walk the City in Paris, New York, Tokyo, Venice and London*. London: Vintage.

Enterkin, J., & Sefton, M. (2006). *A Report on the Exeter Small Claims Mediation Pilot* (DCA Research Series 10/06). London: Department for Constitutional Affairs.

Equality and Human Rights Commission (EHRC). (2008). *The Role and Experience of Inspectorates, Regulators and Complaints-Handling Bodies in Promoting Human Rights Standards in Public Services*. London: Equality and Human Rights Commission.

Equality and Human Rights Commission (EHRC). (2014). *Human Rights in Action: Case Studies for Regulators, Inspectorates and Ombudsmen*. London: Equality and Human Rights Commission.

Equality and Human Rights Commission (EHRC). (2017). *Following Grenfell: The Human Rights and Equality Dimension. Statement from the Equality and Human Rights Commission*.

Etherington, Sir Terence, Master of the Rolls. (2017). Lord Slynn Memorial Lecture, June 2017, on Court Estate and Virtual Hearings. Judiciary of England and Wales.

Feldman, D. (2010). Changes in Human Rights. In M. Adler (Ed.), *Administrative Justice in Context*. Oxford: Hart.

Franca, M. (2018). The Blindness of Justice: An Iconographic Dialogue between Art and Law. In A. Pavoni et al. (Eds.), *Law and the Senses: See*. London: University of Westminster Press.

Fredman, S. (2008). *Human Rights Transformed: Positive Rights and Positive Duties*. Oxford: OUP.

Fredman, S. (2011). *Discrimination Law* (2nd ed.). Oxford: OUP.

Gearty, C. (2006). *Can Human Rights Survive?* Cambridge: CUP.
Gearty, C. (2016). *On Fantasy Island: Britain, Europe and Human Rights.* Oxford: OUP.
Gearty, C., & Mantouvlou, V. (2011). *Debating Social Rights.* Oxford: Hart.
Genn, H., et al. (2007). *Twisting Arms: Court Referred and Court Linked Mediation Under Judicial Pressure* (Research Series 1/07). London: Ministry of Justice.
Gilad, S. (2008). Accountability or Expectations Management? The Role of the Ombudsman in Financial Regulation. *Law & Policy, 30*(2), 227–253.
Gill, C., & Creutzfeldt, N. (2017). The 'Ombuds Watchers': Collective Dissent and Legal Protest Among Users of Public Services Ombuds. *Social & Legal Studies, 27*(3), 367–388.
Gill, C., Mullen, T., & Vivian, N. (2019). *The Managerial Ombuds* (forthcoming).
Gill, C., et al. (2014). *Models of Alternative Dispute Resolution (ADR): A Report for the Legal Ombudsman.* Edinburgh: Queen Margaret University.
Glendon, M. (2001). *A World Made New: Eleanor Roosevelt and the Universal Declaration of Human Rights.* New York: Random House.
Goodhart, D. (2017). *The Road to Somewhere: The Populist Revolt and the Future of Politics.* London: C Hurst & Co.
Greek Ombudsman. (2005). *Annual Report.* Athens: Greek Ombudsman.
Greek Ombudsman. (2007). *Annual Report.* Athens: Greek Ombudsman.
Greek Ombudsman. (2008). *Promoting Equal Treatment: The Greek Ombudsman as National Equality Body.* Athens: Greek Ombudsman.
Greek Ombudsman. (2009). *Equal Treatment of Men and Women in Employment and Labour Relations.* Athens: Greek Ombudsman.
Griffiths, S., & Kippin, H. (2013). Introduction. In H. Kippin et al. (Eds.), *Public Services: A New Reform Agenda.* London: Bloomsbury.
Grindrod, J. (2013). *Concretopia: A Journey around the Rebuilding of Postwar Britain.* Brecon: Old Street Publishing Ltd.
Guinier, L. (2013). Courting the People: Demosprudence and the Law/Politics Divide. *Harvard Law Review, 127*(423), 437–444.
Guinier, L., & Torres, G. (2014). Changing the Wind: Notes towards a Demosprudence of Law and Social Movements. *Yale Law Journal, 123*, 2742–2804.
Gutmann, A., & Thompson, D. (2004). *Why Deliberative Democracy?* Princeton: Princeton University Press.
Halliday, S., & Schmidt, P. (Eds.). (2004). *Human Rights Brought Home: Socio-Legal Perspectives on Human Rights in the National Context.* Oxford: Hart.
Hammarberg, T. (2007a). *Speech to the EU Ombudsmen Network.* Athens, Greece.
Hammarberg, T. (2007b). *Les Droits de l'Homme en Europe: Mission Inaccomplie.* Strasbourg: Council of Europe.
Hampshire, S. (2000). *Justice is Conflict.* Princeton, NJ: Princeton University Press.

Hanley, L. (2017). *Estates: An Intimate History*. London: Granta.
Harlow, C., & Rawlings, R. (1997). *Law and Administration* (2nd ed.). London: Butterworths.
Harlow, C., & Rawlings, R. (2007). Promoting Accountability in Multilevel Governance: A Network Approach. *European Law Journal, 13*, 542–562.
Harris, A. (2010). *Romantic Moderns: English Writers, Artists and the Imagination from Virginia Woolf to John Piper*. London: Thames & Hudson.
Harris, N. (2018). Autonomy, Rights and Children with Special Needs: A New Paradigm? Working Paper 2. *Legislative and Policy Developments in Special Educational Needs in England and Additional Support Needs in Scotland: Advancing Children and Young People's Rights*. Edinburgh and Manchester: Universities of Edinburgh and Manchester.
Hay, C., McKenna, K., & Buck, T. (2010). *Evaluation of Early Neutral Evaluation Alternative Dispute Resolution in the Social Security and Child Support Tribunal* (Ministry of Justice Research Series 2/10). London: Ministry of Justice.
Her Majesty's Courts and Tribunals Service (HMCTS) and Ministry of Justice (MoJ). (2018). Fit for the Future: Transforming the Court and Tribunal Estate. Consultation paper.
Herring, J. (2013a). Forging a Relational Approach: Best Interests or Human Rights? *Medical Law International, 13*(1), 32–54.
Herring, J. (2013b). *Caring and the Law*. Oxford: Hart.
Herring, J. (2017). Compassion, Ethics of Care and Legal Rights. *International Journal of Law in Context, 13*(2), 158–171.
Hertogh, M. (2001). Coercion, Co-operation and Control: Understanding the Policy Impact of Administrative Courts and the Ombudsman in the Netherlands. *Law and Policy, 23*, 47–67.
Hertogh, M. (2013). Why the Ombudsman Does Not Promote Public Trust in Government: Lessons from the Low Countries. *Journal of Social Welfare and Family Law, 35*, 245–258.
Hertogh, M. (2018). *Nobody's Law: Legal Consciousness and Legal Alienation in Everyday Life*. Geneva: Palgrave Macmillan.
Hewart, L. C. J. (1929). *The New Despotism*. London: Ernest Benn.
Higgins, C. (2011, October 10). Tacita Dean's Turbine Hall Film Pays Homage to a Dying Medium. *The Guardian*.
Hilson. (2008). *The Nordic Model: Scandinavia since 1945*. Chicago: Chicago University Press.
Hirschman, A. O. (1970). *Exit, Voice and Loyalty: Responses to Decline in Firms, Organizations, and States*. Cambridge, MA: Harvard University Press.
Holm, N. E. (1995). The Ombudsman—A Gift from Scandinavia to the World. In H. Gammeltoft-Hansen (Ed.), *The Danish Ombudsman*. Copenhagen: The Danish Ombudsman.
Horwitz, M. (1977). The Rule of Law: An Unqualified Human Good? *Yale Law Journal, 86*, 561–566.

Howard, E. (1965). *Garden Cities of To-Morrow*. Cambridge, MA: MIT Press.
Hunt, P. (2017). *Social Rights are Human Rights—But the UK System is Rigged*. London: Centre for Welfare Reform.
Hurwitz, S. (1960, May 12). Interview with H W R Wade and J A G Griffiths. *The Listener*.
Immigration Law Practitioners Group (ILPA). (2019). EU Settled Status Automated Data Checks—ILPA Research Piece. Retrieved February 23, 2019, from http://www.ilpa.org.uk/resources.php/35100/eu-settled-status-automated-data-checks-ilpa-research-piece-30-january-2019
Irvine, C., & Farrington, L. (2016). Mediation and Emotions: Perception and Regulation. In J. Stannard & H. Conway (Eds.), *The Emotional Dynamics of Law and Legal Discourse*. Oxford: Bloomsbury Professional.
Jackson, A. (2002). From Solving Problems to Selling Product: The Changing Role of Designers in Post-war Britain. Designing Britain 1945–1975. University of Brighton. Retrieved February 18, 2019, from https://vads.ac.uk/learning/designingbritain/html/crd_desref.html
Jacobs, J. (2000). *The Death and Life of Great American Cities*. London: Pimlico.
Judt, T. (2005). *Postwar: A History of Europe since 1945*. London: William Heinemann.
Karydis, V. (2011). *The Greek Equality Body in the Spotlight*. Brussels: Equinet.
Khilnani, S., Raghavan, V., & Thiruvengadam, A. (2012). Revisiting the Role of the Judiciary in Plural Societies. In S. Khilnani, V. Raghavan, & A. Thiruvengadam (Eds.), *Comparative Constitutionalism in South Asia*. New Delhi: OUP.
King, J. (2012). *Judging Social Rights*. Cambridge: CUP.
King, M. (2018). *Speech to the Annual Conference of the Ombudsman Association*. Edinburgh.
Kirkham, R., & Martin, J. (2014). Designing an English Public Services Ombudsman. *Journal of Social Welfare and Family Law, 36*(3), 330–448.
Klein, A. (2007). Judging as Nudging: New Governance Approaches for the Enforcement of Constitutional Social and Economic Rights. *Columbia Human Rights Law Review, 39*, 351–422.
Klug, F. (2000). *Values for a Godless Age: The Story of the United Kingdom's New Bill of Rights*. Harmondsworth: Penguin.
Kucsko-Stadlmayer, G. (Ed.). (2008). *European Ombudsman-Institutions*. Vienna: Springer.
Labour Party. (1964). *The New Britain*. London: Labour Party.
Lam, S. M. (2018). Alvar Aalto—Bringing Well-being to 'The Little Man'. *V&A Library* blog. Retrieved from https://www.vam.ac.uk/blog/.
Laverty, P., & Loach, K. (2016). *I, Daniel Blake*. Pontefract: Route Publishing.
Law Commission. (2011). *Public Services Ombudsmen* (Report No. 329). London: Law Commission.

Le Sueur, A. (2016). Robot Government: Automated Decision-Making and Its Implications for Parliament. In A. Horne & A. Le Sueur (Eds.), *Parliament: Legislation and Accountability*. Oxford: Hart Publishing.

Leggatt, S. A. (2001). *Tribunals for Users—One System, One Service*. London: Stationery Office.

Levi-Strauss, C. (1966). *The Savage Mind*. Chicago: Chicago University Press.

Local Government Ombudsman (LGO). (2008). *Report on an Investigation into Complaint Nos 06/A/16993, 06/A/16997 and 06/A/17360 against Basildon District Council*. London: LGO.

Local Government Ombudsman (LGO). (2014). *Special Educational Needs: Preparing for the Future*. London: LGO.

Local Government Ombudsman and Parliamentary and Health Service Ombudsman (LGO and PHSO). (2008). *Injustice in Residential Care: A Joint Report by the Local Government Ombudsman and Health Service Ombudsman for England*. HC Paper No. 421, Session 2007/08. London: The Stationery Office.

Local Government Ombudsman and Parliamentary and Health Service Ombudsman (LGO and PHSO). (2009). *Six Lives: The Provision of Public Services to People with Learning Disabilities*. HC Paper No. 203, Session 2008/09. London: The Stationery Office.

Local Government and Social Care Ombudsman (LGSCO). (2017). *Education, Health and Care Plans: Our First 100 Investigations*. London: LGSCO.

Local Government and Social Care Ombudsman (LGSCO). (2018a). *Annual Report 2017–18*. London: LGSCO.

Local Government and Social Care Ombudsman (LGSCO). (2018b). *Under Pressure—The Impact of the Changing Environment on Local Government Complaints*. London: LGSCO.

Mae Architects. (2014). *Places for Strangers: Ideas for Places, People and the City* (S. Bose, Ed.). Zurich: Park Books.

Malik, C. (1968). Introduction. In O. Nolde (Ed.), *Free and Equal: Human Rights in Ecumenical Perspective*. Geneva: World Council of Churches.

Manzini, E. (2015). *Design, When Everybody Designs: An Introduction to Design for Social Innovation*. Cambridge, MA: MIT Press.

Marin, A. (2006). Innovate or Perish. *Canadian Journal of Administrative Law and Practice, 20*, 101–115.

Marshall, T. H. (1992). Citizenship and Social Class. In T. H. Marshall & T. Bottomore (Eds.), *Citizenship and Social Class*. London: Pluto.

Mashaw, J. (1983). *Bureaucratic Justice: Managing Social Security Disability Claims*. New Haven: Yale University Press.

Mason, P. (2017). Foreword. In P. Hunt (Ed.), *Social Rights are Human Rights*. London: Centre for Welfare Reform.

May, C. (2015). Mediating Court of Protection Cases—Summary of Research. *UK Administrative Justice Institute (UKAJI)* blog.

McCarthy, F. (1972). *All Things Bright & Beautiful: Design in Britain 1830 to Today*. London: George Allen & Unwin Ltd.

McCarthy, F. (1982). *British Design Since 1880: A Visual History*. London: Lund Humphries.

McCarthy, F. (2014). *Anarchy & Beauty: William Morris and His Legacy 1960–1960*. London: National Portrait Gallery.

McCormick, M. (2014). Changing Times, Changing Designs: Council Offices Then and Now. *Failed Architecture* blog.

McGregor, et al. (2017). *National Human Rights Institutions in Europe and dispute Resolution: A Mapping*. Oxford Brookes University, University of Essex and University of Bristol.

McMillan, J. (2009). *The Ombudsman's Role in Human Rights Protection—An Australian Perspective*. Paper to the Eleventh Asian Ombudsman Association Conference, Bangkok, 2–5 November 2009.

Menkel-Meadow, C. (2002). When Litigation is Not the Only Way: Consensus Building and Mediation as Public Interest Lawyering. *Washington University Journal of Law and Policy, 10*, 37–62.

Menkel-Meadow, C (2004/2005). The Lawyer's Role(s) in Deliberative Democracy. *Nevada Law Journal, 5*, 347–369.

Menkel-Meadow, C. (2006, Winter). Deliberative Democracy and Conflict Resolution: Two Theories and Practices of Participation in the Polity. *Dispute Resolution Magazine*, pp. 18–22.

Menkel-Meadow, C. (2011). Scaling Up Deliberative Democracy as Dispute Resolution in Healthcare Reform: A Work in Progress. *Law and Contemporary Problems, 74*(1), 1–30.

Menkel-Meadow, C. (2016). *Mediation and Its Applications for Good Decision-Making and Dispute Resolution* (K. U. Leuven, Ed.). Cambridge: Intersentia Ltd.

Ministry of Justice. (2017a). Tribunals and Gender Recognition Certificate Statistics Quarterly July–September 2017.

Ministry of Justice. (2017b). SEND Appeal Rates 2014–2017. SEND Tribunal Tables: Statistics on the Appeal Rate to the SEND Tribunal.

Ministry of Justice. (2018a). HM Courts and Tribunals Service: Citizen User Experience Research. HMCTS Customer Insight Team.

Ministry of Justice. (2018b). Tribunals and Gender Recognition Certificate Statistics Quarterly April–June 2018.

Minton, A. (2012). *Ground Control: Fear and Happiness in the Twenty-First-Century City*. London: Penguin Books.

Morris Jones, W. H. (1949). *Socialism and Bureaucracy*. London: Fabian Society.

Moyn, S. (2018). *Not Enough: Human Rights in an Unequal World*. Cambridge, MA: Harvard University Press.

Mulcahy, L. (2011). *Legal Architecture: Justice, Due Process and the Place of Law*. London: Routledge.

Mulcahy, L. (2013). The Collective Interest in Private Dispute Resolution. *Oxford Journal of Legal Studies, 33*, 59–80.
Mullen, T. (2017). Access to Justice in Administrative Law and Administrative Justice. In E. Palmer et al. (Eds.), *Austerity and Access to Justice*. London: Bloomsbury.
Mussari, M. (2016). *Danish Modern: Between Art and Design*. London: Bloomsbury.
Narkiewicz-Laine, C. (undated). Good Design is a Human Right: An Essay that Commemorates the 65th Anniversary of Good Design. *Chicago Athenaeum Museum of Architecture and Design*.
Nason, S. (2015). Understanding Administrative Justice in Wales: Full Report Including Executive Summary. Bangor University, Committee for Administrative Justice and Tribunals Wales. *UK Administrative Justice Institute (UKAJI)* blog.
Nason, S. (2018). *Administrative Justice: Wales' First Devolved Justice System: Evaluation and Recommendations*. Bangor University.
National Audit Office. (2018a). *Comptroller and Auditor General, Financial Sustainability of Local Authorities 2018*. HC 834 Session 2017–2019. London: National Audit Office.
National Audit Office. (2018b). *Handling of the Windrush Situation*. HC 1622 Session 2017–2019. London: National Audit Office.
Newton, L. (2010). *House of Lords Hansard*, 29 November 2010, Col. 1325.
Nonet, P., & Selznick, P. (1978). *Toward Responsive Law: Law and Society in Transition*. New York: Harper Torch.
Northern Ireland Ombudsman. (2016). *Human Rights Manual*. Belfast: Northern Ireland Ombudsman and Northern Ireland Human Rights Commission.
Nussbaum, M. (2004). *Hiding from Humanity: Disgust, Shame, and the Law*. Princeton: Princeton University Press.
Nussbaum, M. (2011). *Creating Capabilities: The Human Development Approach*. Cambridge, MA: Harvard University Press.
Nussbaum, M. (2013). *Political Emotions: Why Love Matters for Justice*. Cambridge, MA: Harvard University Press.
Nussbaum, M. (2018). *The Monarchy of Fear: A Philosopher Looks at our Political Crisis*. Oxford: OUP.
O'Brien, N. (2009, July). Ombudsmen and Social Rights Adjudication. *Public Law*, pp. 466–478.
O'Brien, N. (2011). Law and "The Good Life": Learning Disability, Equality and Healthcare in the UK. *The Equal Rights Review, 6*, 83–96.
O'Brien, N. (2012). Administrative Justice Libertarian Cinderella in Search of an Egalitarian Prince. *Political Quarterly, 83*(3), 494–501.
O'Brien, N. (2016). Disability Discrimination Law in the United Kingdom and the New Civil Rights History: The Contribution of Caroline Gooding. *Journal of Law and Society, 43*(3), 444–468.

O'Brien, N. (2017). Administrative Justice in the Wake of 'I, Daniel Blake'. *Political Quarterly, 89*(1), 82–91.

O'Brien, N. (2018). Ombudsmen and Public Authorities: A Modest Proposal. In M. Hertogh & R. Kirkham (Eds.), *Research Handbook on The Ombudsman*. Cheltenham: Edward Elgar.

O'Brien, N., & Thompson, B. (2010). Human Rights Accountability in the UK: Deliberative Democracy and the Role of the Ombudsman. *European Human Rights Law Review, 5*, 504–512.

O'Cinneide, C. (2018). The Social Security (Scotland) Act 2018—A Rights-Based Approach to Social Security? *Edinburgh Law Review, 23*, 123–130.

O'Donnell, G. (2007). *Dissonances: Democratic Critiques of Democracy*. Notre Dame, IN: University of Notre Dame.

O'Hara, G. (2008a). The Intellectuals' Ideal: British Views of Scandinavia in the 1950s and 1960s. In J. E. Myhre (Ed.), *Intellectuals in the Public Sphere in Britain and Norway after World War II*. Oslo: Oslo Academic Press.

O'Hara, G. (2008b). Applied Socialism of a Fairy Moderate Kind. *Scandinavian Journal of History, 33*(1), 1–25.

O'Hara, G. (2012). *Governing Post-war Britain: The Paradoxes of Progress*. Geneva: Palgrave Macmillan.

Office of the Independent Adjudicator (OIA). (2013). *Mediation—A Guide for Students*. Reading: OIA.

O'Neill, O. (2018). *A Question of Trust: The BBC Reith Lectures 2002*. Cambridge: CUP.

Pamuk, O. (2013, June/July). A Modest Manifesto for Museums. *American Craft Magazine*.

Parliamentary and Health Service Ombudsman (PHSO). (2018). *Annual Report 2017–18*.

Pavoni, A., et al. (Eds.). (2018). *Law and the Senses: See*. London: University of Westminster Press.

Pearce, B., & Stubbs, M. (2000). The Role of Mediation in the Settlement of Planning Disputes at Appeal: The Debate and Research Agenda. *Environment and Planning, 32*, 1335–1358.

Pegram, T. (2008). Accountability in Hostile Times: The Case of the Peruvian Human Rights Ombudsman 1996–2001. *Journal of Latin American Studies, 40*, 51–82.

Pegram, T. (2013). The Bolivian Human Rights Ombudsman and Economic, Social and Cultural Rights. In E. Brems, G. de Beco, & W. Vandenhole (Eds.), *National Human Rights Institutions, and Economic, Social and Cultural Rights*. Antwerp: Intersentia.

Perlin, M. (2013). *"The Ladder of the Law Has No Top and No Bottom": How Therapeutic Jurisprudence Can Give Life to International Human Rights*. Paper based on remarks given at the Congress of the International Academy of Law and Mental Health, Amsterdam.

Peruzzotti, E. (2012). The Societalization of Horizontal Accountability: Rights Advocacy and the Defensor del Pueblo de la Nacion in Argentina. In R. Goodman & T. Pegram (Eds.), *Human Rights, State Compliance, and Social Change*. Cambridge: CUP.

Price, K. (2018). Designing a New Welcome Experience at the V&A. *V&A* blog. Retrieved from https://www.vam.ac.uk/blog/.

Prisons and Probation Ombudsman. (2013). Learning Lessons Bulletin. *Complaints Investigations Issue 2—Religion*.

Pritchard, H. (2017). Tribunal Reform in Wales under the Wales Act 2017. *UK Administrative Justice Institute (UKAJI)* blog.

Project for Public Spaces. (undated). Eleven Principles for Creating Great Community Places. *Project for Public Spaces* blog.

Public Administration Select Committee (PASC). (2014). Time for a People's Ombudsman. *Fourteenth Report of Session 2013–14*. London: House of Commons.

Ramesh, R. (2013, May 1). Equity Not Equality—Interview with Danielle Allen. *The Guardian*, p. 35.

Ranchordás, S. (2018). Cities as Corporations? The Privatization of Cities and the Automation of Local Law. *Oxford Business Law* blog.

Ray, B. (2011). Demosprudence in Comparative Perspective. *Stanford Journal of International Law, 47*, 111–173.

Richards, Z. (2019). *Responsive Legality: The New Administrative Justice*. Abingdon and New York: Routledge.

Richardson, G., & Genn, H. (2007). Tribunals in Transition: Resolution or Adjudication. *Public Law*, pp. 116–141.

Rogers, R. (2017). *A Place for All People*. Edinburgh: Canongate.

Roosevelt, E. (1948). The Promise of Human Rights. *Foreign Affairs*. In A. Black (Ed.), *Courage in a Dangerous World: The Political Writings of Eleanor Roosevelt* (pp. 156–168). New York: Columbia University Press.

Roosevelt, E. (1958). *The Great Question*. Remarks delivered at the United Nations. New York: United Nations.

Roosevelt, E. (2016). *The Moral Basis of Democracy*. New York: Open Road.

Rosanvallon, P. (2008). *Counter-Democracy: Politics in an Age of Distrust*. Cambridge: CUP.

Russell, G. (1949). What is Good Design? *Design* 1, pp. 2–6. London: Design Council.

Russell, J. (2014). *Peggy Angus: Designer, Teacher, Painter*. Eastbourne: Antiques Collectors' Club/Towner.

Ryder, E. (2016). The Modernisation of Access to Justice in Times of Austerity. *5th Annual Ryder Lecture*. The University of Bolton.

Ryder, E. (2018). *The Modernisation of Tribunals 2018: A Report by the Senior President of Tribunals*. London: HMCTS.

Sabel, C., & Simon, W. (2004). Destabilization Rights: How Public Law Litigation Succeeds. *Harvard Law Review, 117*, 1016–1101.

Sachs, A. (2007). The South African Experience—Interview with Martin Crick. In *DRC Legal Achievements 2000–2007*. London: Disability Rights Commission.
Sachs, A. (2009). *The Strange Alchemy of Life and Law*. Oxford: OUP.
Schiavone, A. (2012). *The Invention of Law in the West*. Cambridge, MA: Harvard.
Scottish Government. (2009). *A Guide to the Use of Mediation in the Planning System in Scotland*. Edinburgh: Scottish Government.
Scraton, P. (2013). The Legacy of Hillsborough: liberating Truth, Challenging Power. *Race & Class, 55*(2), 1–27.
Sennett, R. (2003). *Respect: The Formation of Character in an Age of Inequality*. New York: W W Norton & Company.
Sennett, R. (2018). *Building and Dwelling*. London: Allen Lane.
Shonfield, A. (1965). *Modern Capitalism: The Changing Balance of Public and Private Power*. London: OUP.
Simon, W. (2004). Solving Problems v Claiming Rights: The Pragmatist Challenge to Legal Liberalism. *William and Mary Law Review, 46*, 127–212.
Simon, W. (2009). The Warren Court, Legalism and Democracy: Sketch for a Critique in a Style Learned from Morton Horwitz. *Columbia Law School, Public Law and Legal Theory Working Group Paper No. 09-196*.
Simpson, M., McKeever, G., & Gray, A. M. (2017). *Social Security Systems Based on Dignity and Respect*. Equality and Human Rights Commission. Retrieved February 18, 2019, from https://www.equalityhumanrights.com/sites/default/files/social_security_systems_based_on_dignity_and_respect.pdf
Solnit, R. (2002). *Wanderlust: A History of Walking*. London: Granta.
Sontag, S. (2003). *Regarding the Pain of Others*. London: Penguin Books.
Sossin, L. (2017). Designing Administrative Justice. *Windsor Yearbook of Access to Justice, 34*(1), 87–111.
Spanou, C. (2013). *The Greek Ombudsman and Public Administration during Challenging Times*. 13th Annual Lecture of the Hellenic Observatory, European Institute, London School of Economics, 25 November 2013. Retrieved from www.macropolis.gr.
Stacey, F. (1971). *The British Ombudsman*. Oxford: Clarendon Press.
Street, H. (1975). *Justice in the Welfare State* (Hamlyn Lecture, 20th series) (2nd ed.). London: Stevens.
Sugarman, D. (1986). Legal Theory, the Common Law Mind and the Making of the Textbook Tradition. In W. Twining (Ed.), *Legal Theory and Common Law*. Oxford: Blackwell.
Sunstein, C. (2004). *The Second Bill of Rights: FDR's Unfinished Revolution and Why We Need It More Than Ever*. New York: Basic Books.
Tangley, L. (1965). *Law for a New World?* (Hamlyn Lecture, 17th series). London: Stevens.
Terrett, B. (2012a). A Few Notes on Typography. *GDS* Blog.
Terrett, B. (2012b). Ben Terrett on designing GOV.UK. *GDS* Blog.

Thomas, R. (2011). *Speech to the Administrative Justice and Tribunals Council Annual Conference*, 17 November 2011. Administrative Justice and Tribunals Council.

Thomas, R., & Tomlinson, J. (2016). *Current Issues in Administrative Justice: Examining Administrative Review, Better Initial Decisions, and Tribunal Reform*. Sheffield and Manchester: Universities of Sheffield and Manchester.

Thomas, R., & Tomlinson, J. (2017). Mapping Current Issues in Administrative Justice: Austerity and the 'More Bureaucratic Rationality' Approach. *Journal of Social Welfare and Family Law, 39*(3), 380–399.

Titmuss, R. (1971). Welfare 'Rights', Law and Discretion. *Political Quarterly, 42*, 113–132.

Tomkins, A. (2005). *Our Republican Constitution*. Oxford: Hart.

Tomlinson, J. (2017a). The Grammar of Administrative Justice Values. *Journal of Social Welfare and Family Law, 39*(4), 524–537.

Tomlinson, J. (2017b). The Policy and Politics of Building Tribunals for a Digital Age: How 'Design Thinking' is Shaping the Future of the Public Law System. *UK Constitutional Law* blog.

Tomlinson, J. (2019). Brexit and Administrative Justice: An Early Analysis (Part II—Emerging Trends). *UK Administrative Justice Institute (UKAJI)* blog.

Tomlinson, J., & Thomas, R. (2018). *The Digitalisation of Tribunals: What We Know and What We Need to Know*. London: Public Law Project and UK Administrative Justice Institute.

Toth, G. (2009). Where the Sidewalk Doesn't End. *Project for Public Spaces* blog.

Tyndall, P., Mitchell, C., & Gill, C. (2018). *Value for Money*. London: PHSO.

UK Administrative Justice Institute (UKAJI). (2018). *A Research Roadmap for Administrative Justice*. Colchester: University of Essex.

Vanhala, L. (2011). *Making Rights a Reality? Disability Rights Activists and Legal Mobilization*. Cambridge: CUP.

Vitale, D. (2018). A Trust Network Model for Social Rights. *Oxford Journal of Legal Studies, 2018*, 1–27.

White Paper: *Transforming Public Services: Complaints, Redress and Tribunals*. (2004). London: Department for Constitutional Affairs.

Whyatt, S. J. (1961). *The Citizen and the Administration: The Redress of Grievances*. London: Stevens & Sons.

Williams, R. (1961). *The Long Revolution*. London: Chatto and Windus.

Williams, R. (2018). Rethinking Deference for Algorithmic Decision-making. *Oxford Legal Studies Research Paper No. 7/2019*.

Winner, L. (1980). Do Artifacts Have Politics? *Daedalus, 109*(1), 121–136.

Woodham, J. M. (1997). *Twentieth-Century Design*. Oxford: Oxford University Press.

Yallop, J. (2015). *Dreamstreets: A Journey through Britain's Village Utopias*. London: Vintage.

Zacka, B. (2017). *When the State Meets the Street: Public Service and Moral Agency*. Cambridge, MA: Harvard University Press.

Index

M. Doyle, N. O'Brien, *Reimagining Administrative Justice*,
https://doi.org/10.1007/978-3-030-21388-6

The manufacturer's authorised representative in the EU is Springer Nature Customer Service Centre GmbH, Europaplatz 3, 69115 Heidelberg, Germany. If you have any concerns regarding our products, please contact ProductSafety@springernature.com

Printed and bound by CPI Group (UK) Ltd, Croydon, CR0 4YY
05/10/2026
02228155-0003